Nick Williams left a successful job in IT sales and marketing to follow his heart. He is now a world expert on inspiration at work. He has coached thousands of people around the world to greater fulfilment, happiness and success in what they do. The author of five books including *How To Be Inspired* and the internationally best selling *The Work We Were Born To Do,* he works with individuals, entrepreneurs and organisations to help them achieve peak performance through inspiration, passion and fulfilment. His work has inspired such diverse groups as lawyers, teachers, chief executives, the unemployed, entrepreneurs, doctors, nurses and the clergy as well as leaders in the media, entertainment and business world. His work has been the subject of over 800 media features. His website is www.nick-williams.com

To Be.
Be inspired!,
much love
Nick
x.

How To Be
INSPIRED

NICK WILLIAMS

Foreword by Barbara J. Winter

Sogna Bella

Sogna Bella

Copyright © Nick Williams 2005

A CIP catalogue record for this book
is available from the British Library

ISBN 10: 1-905806-03-5
ISBN 13: 978-1-905806-03-4

Printed and Bound by Butler & Tanner,
Frome, Somerset

Tree of Life Publishing
PO Box 12036, Bromsgrove
Worcs., B60 1WT

When you work only for yourself, or for your own personal gain, your mind will seldom rise above the limitations of an undeveloped personal life. But when you are inspired by some great purpose, some extraordinary project, all your thoughts break your bonds: your mind transcends limitations, your consciousness expands in every direction, and find you yourself in a new, great and wonderful world. Dormant forces, faculties and talents become alive and you discover yourself to be a greater person by far than you ever dreamed yourself to be.

Patanjali, founder of Yoga sutras, 2nd century BC

Contents

Acknowledgements

I'd like to dedicate this book to my father Harold who, at 85 and with failing health, is still a great source of love, encouragement and inspiration to me.

I also want to thank my partner Helen for her continuing love and support; and to my mum, Pam. Also Maggy Whitehouse and Peter Dickinson for allowing me to publish this book and making it happen. Continuing thanks to Barbara Winter, my soul friend and partner in inspiration, and to Niki Hignett our friend, technology guru and business partner. Continuing gratitude to Steve Nobel and my family of friends at Alternatives. Thanks to Rick Thorn for inspiring me to new possibilities, to John Greig and Gabriella Goddard for their support. And to Julia McCutchen for her friendship and support and Jackee for being a soul sister and friend. Thanks also to Jeff Allen, Julie Wookey and all at Psychology of Vision for being friends on the journey. Thanks yet again to Adam Stern, Matt Ingrams and Martin Wenner for their presence in my life over the last ten years.

Finally, I feel so blessed when a source of inspiration comes into my life and truly helps to transform it. For that, I am deeply grateful to Steven Pressfield for writing *The War of Art* and reminding me that being a spiritual warrior and a servant of the mystery is the only thing that really gives life meaning. Steven, for your writing and your generosity of time and heart when we met, thank you so much.

And *A Course in Miracles* continues to be my guiding light—thank you.

Foreword

by Barbara J. Winter

On a sunny January morning in 2002, Nick Williams and I set up shop on a beach near Santa Barbara, California to do a bit of brainstorming. At first we had this quiet and lovely place all to ourselves but, as the day progressed, more people came to the beach to picnic or spend time with their friends and family. A little boy nearby began chasing seagulls. 'I guess he hasn't learned that when you chase something, it runs away,' said Nick. 'If he'd just stand still with his hand out holding a piece of bread, the birds would come to him.'

'What a great reminder,' I thought. Then, just in case I didn't get the message, another family showed up with food for the birds. Within seconds, dozens of seagulls and pigeons appeared out of nowhere to gobble the bits of food.

The other great reminder in this little incident is that when you hang out with inspired people, you start to see that inspiration is all around. It's omnipresent and it's free for the taking. I don't know about you but for me that's a new revelation.

For most of my life, when I thought about inspiration (which I didn't do very often) I believed it was something you either had or didn't. Like red hair or brown eyes, a few people got the gift of inspiration. Those with massive talent like Leonardo da Vinci or Bach were obviously both talented and inspired but the most that the rest of us could hope for were random and infrequent moments when we soared a little. With a belief system like that, there wasn't much point in thinking about inspiration since it seemed rare and wouldn't be part of my life.

Then, thirty-some years ago, I discovered the world of motivation. I read motivational books, went to seminars and success rallies. If I couldn't be inspired, perhaps I could whip myself into a motivated frenzy. I learned slogans. I set outlandish goals. I got swept up in the emotional whirlwind in auditoria listening to secular evangelists. A few days later, I'd beat myself up when I couldn't maintain a constant state of enthusiasm.

Now I know that motivational thinking, as it is popularly practised, should be called Synthetic Inspiration. It bears almost no resemblance to the real thing. I'm not sure when I came to realise the difference between motivation and inspiration but, now that I can tell them apart, I don't want the fake stuff when the real thing is available.

Nick Williams has taught me more about inspiration than anyone I know. I've learned that it's essential always to have paper and pen close at hand when we're together because an avalanche of ideas is inevitable. I've learned that inspiration—unlike motivation—isn't noisy. Nick often says the wisest things in the quietest voice. I've learned that being in the company of an inspired person fires my own creative spirit. I've learned that inspiration makes life sweet, makes problems manageable, keeps things interesting. In both big and little ways, Nick has shown me that inspiration begets inspiration. And now he's going to show you, too.

I used to have a poster near my front door that read, 'It's not where you're going ... it's where you're coming from.' While that might sound like a bit of leftover jargon from the sixties, it also bears a truth that touches us all. Any project, any goal, any relationship with which we're involved is coloured by what we bring to it. What Nick brings to this book is a fresh understanding of the power of inspiration—and its abundance.

This insightful collection of thoughts on inspiration comes straight out of Nick's own experience in uncovering the secrets to this some-what mystical phenomenon. While it may be mystical, it's not unreachable. You have only to look at Nick's life, at his teaching, his sense of adventure, his willingness to grow and evolve, to know that inspiration isn't just an interesting concept. As Nick demonstrates, it can be an everyday event.

Nick explores inspiration from every angle. Even better, he shows us how inspiration can be a constant companion, guiding us closer to the life of our dreams. In the end, of course, inspiration belongs to those who are actively working on a dream. Since it's impossible to have too much inspiration, consider this your handbook for making every moment a new adventure in inspired living. 'Good things as well as bad are caught by a kind of infection,' C.S. Lewis reminds us. ' If you want to get warm you must stand near the fire; if you want to get wet you must get into the water. If you want joy, power, peace, eternal life, you must get close to, or even into, the thing that has them ... They are a great fountain of energy and beauty spurting up at the very centre of reality. If you are close to it, the spray will wet you; if you are not, you will remain dry.'

And if you want inspiration to be at the centre of your life, keep reading the book that's in your hands right now.

Barbara Winter, Minneapolis, USA, March 2005

Introduction

Often we don't know how thirsty we are until we have a drink and, similarly, we often don't know how much we need inspiration until we experience it. On the whole we live in such a world cut off from spirit that we take that to be normal. That's how it was for me when I discovered personal development in my late 20s; my soul screamed with delight and felt I had come home. But I didn't want inspiration as a weekend or evening only activity, I wanted it to be at the heart and the centre of my life. But at the time I was selling computers and bored with it. After years of inner battle, I finally left the corporate world to follow that inner voice and sense of inspiration and to make my life the living answer to a single question: *What happens when I put inspiration at the centre of my life?* My life is still the evolving answer to that question.

I have discovered that inspiration is a powerful, tangible force, a phenomenon that can draw us forward for our whole lives. Most of us have glimpses of inspiration: on a weekend seminar; after reading a book that touches and resonates with us; having been in the presence of someone who is themselves inspired; as the result of a brainstorming session with a friend; after a coaching session; when we have some personal crisis and resolve not to shelve our dreams any longer. Equally, we also know the experience of that inspiration gradually petering out and returning to the uninspired state of inertia that may have characterised our lives. Or maybe we got going with an inspired venture only to find our energy draining to zero.

That was certainly my experience. I could go on a weekend workshop and come home determined to change my life and then, within a few days, have sunk back into despair again. But gradually I have learned that inspiration need not be occasional but can be perpetual. I have learned, and am still learning, how to build my life around my inspiration, to have my life be an expression of that inspiration. I have learned a lot and probably unlearned even more. In this book I want to share what I have learned about living a life of inspiration, what works and what will defeat us.

In its natural state, I believe our minds are perpetually inspired because in our essence we are spirit. Inspiration reconnects us to the awe and wonder of life. A large part of our job is to unshackle our minds from the bonds in which we have put them. Inspiration wants us to graduate beyond the protestant work ethic of pain, struggle and sacrifice and into creativity and ease. Inspiration is a call to partner with the divine. This book will help you create success through inspiration, not perspiration. Hard work alone will not make us successful and happy. Inspired ideas, passion, joy will give meaning to our lives, growing us and leading us forward.

This book was a wonderful example of how easy inspiration can be; it just flowed out of me, the majority of it within a three-week period over Christmas and New Year 2004/2005. I was pregnant with it and it was an easy birth. I hope you enjoy reading it as much I loved writing it.

Nick Williams, London, March 2005

Section One:
Nurturing inspiration

Inspiration is perpetually available to us. Our job is not to 'get it' but to nurture our receptivity to it.

Secret number 1

Inspired people know their own wells of inspiration

Perpetual inspiration is as necessary to the life of goodness, holiness and happiness as perpetual respiration is necessary to animal life.
William Law

It sounds so simple but it is profound—inspired people know what inspires them and, if they don't know, they are willing to invest time and energy discovering. But did you have someone around you every day, at home or school saying to you, 'One of the most important things in life is that you be inspired and know what inspires you and then follow that sense of inspiration? Being inspired is a tremendous power, so get to discover your own sources of inspiration and nurture your inspiration.' I doubt it; most of us didn't. So we can too easily end up sidelining our sense of inspiration and may have a distant relationship with inspiration or think it's reserved for special people. To be regularly inspired we have to re-acquaint or even simply acquaint ourselves with our own wells and sources of inspiration. To be regularly inspired, we need to take responsibility for putting more uplifting ideas, thoughts and beliefs into our minds and hearts. The world is full of so many different kinds of inspiration and beauty.

So who and what does inspire you? What uplifts you? What nourishes you spiritually? We are all inspired by different things so our work is to remember and discover what our own sources are. There are very few things or people that inspire everybody so our work is to get to know *the shape of our own souls*. We need to acquaint ourselves with the things that we are naturally drawn to, fascinated by, in awe of, curious about and uplifted by. For some of us it's areas of nature, sporting achievements, business, selfless service, charitable giving, science, art, fashion, creativity, poetry, travel, film, music, forgiveness, love or spirituality. Healthily inspired people don't limit their sources of inspiration, they allow themselves diverse and varied sources.

So here's the secret: Inspired people get to know and become intimate with their own wells of inspiration.

So what films, people, music, places, literature, stories, forms of creativity, entrepreneurs or spiritual teachers inspire you? Who makes you feel good about yourself? Who is most affirming of you? Who are your role-models of inspiration? What makes you glad to be alive? What do you experience as the pinnacle of living? If the answers to those questions don't come easily to you, take it on as a wonderfully powerful project. Inspired people spend time at their wells of inspiration, filling up regularly so they keep their souls aloft and generate new ideas. Being inspired is about knowing where our own wells are.

Secret number 2

Inspired people go to their wells of inspiration daily

One ought, every day at least, to hear a little song, read a good poem, see a fine picture and, if it were possible, to speak a few reasonable words.
J. W. von Goethe

Inspiration isn't a single event, it's a daily activity. I was running a seminar for managers in an NHS trust in the west of England and we were talking about inspiration at work and keeping our souls aloft. One of the participants said to the group, 'My wife and I love dancing. It's how we met and what we've always loved and shared. Yet with our two young children, we haven't been dancing for several years.' His comment reminded me how it's only half the equation to know where our wells of inspiration are and it's equally important to make sure we make the time and energy to go to them regularly.

Because most of us have not been educated in the importance of inspiration to a healthy life, we tend to relegate inspiration and creativity to the bottom of our *to do* list, if they are even on there at all. My friend Barbara Winter has an expression; she says, 'Inspiration is not vaccination.' She means that we don't just get inspired once and then we are done for the next five years. We need to nurture inspiration on a daily, even hourly basis. Inspiration is incredibly powerful and still needs regular renewal and nourishment to sustain it.

When I was still in my corporate career, I would go off on a week-end personal development workshop and come home Sunday night totally clear and inspired, knowing my way forward. I'd go back to work Monday morning and, within a day or two, I would feel depressed and hopeless again. I had not learned to maintain and sustain inspiration. I still thought inspiration was rare rather than being a daily occurrence. I had not learned how to build a community for myself around inspiration. One of the things with which I have really needed to make peace is how much I do need to nurture inspiration. To live the kind of life I want to live, I spend a lot of time, energy and money nurturing my inspiration and keeping my soul aloft.

In cultures that value hard work and sacrifice highly, we can easily relegate inspiration to very low priority, even judging it as a luxury and indulgence. We can even be rather proud of ourselves for having slipped creative work in there between domestic chores and financial obligations. But we need to raise the importance, the priority of inspiration in our lives. It is important and urgent every day and we need to put it at the top of the *to be* list. Life without inspiration is mere survival and getting by.

I recently returned from running a seminar with Barbara in Las Vegas. Despite my tiredness and jet lag, I felt uplifted and was wondering about why that was. The seminar and the delegates were great fun and I sensed there was something more. Then I realised that in my six days there, I had been to see two *Cirque du Soleil* shows, another show, a fantastic and ground-breaking film called *What the Bleep* and also had a lively meal with the seminar delegates at a Moroccan restaurant. In London, I would be surprised if I gave myself that much entertainment in three months, let alone a week! I realised how I had judged entertainment to be a luxury rather than a necessity. When I recognised how my soul flourished on the fun and entertainment and immersing myself in the creativity and life-energy of others, I immediately booked a couple of shows in London.

So here's the secret: Inspiration needs to become a habit, not a single event.

Going to our wells can be a free and immediate activity too; playing our favourite music, watching our favourite films on DVD, spending time with our favourite friends or reading our favourite poetry. It is more about willingness and choice than it is about spending money.

Secret number 3

Inspired people get inspiring input

To serve the human race in the largest and highest sense, we must bring forth into living expression the truest, the best and the greatest that we can possibly find in the depths of our own sublime beings. And to this end we need all the inspiration we can receive from nature, all the love and friendship we can receive from man and all the wisdom and power we can receive from God.
Christian D. Larson

It's hard, if not impossible, to be inspired in isolation. We get inspiration from people, the world and the natural world around us. I know that when I got involved with Alternatives, initially as a volunteer then latterly as a director, it served a wonderful purpose for me. Every week, sometimes several times a week, I got inspirational input. I got to hear, meet and experience some of the best known, and some lesser known, people in the worlds of personal and spiritual development, environmental issues, creativity, love and health. It was like having a university education in possibility rather than limitation. As the old computer adage goes, *GIGO*—garbage in, garbage out. So I began slowly to experience *IIIO*; inspiration in, inspiration out. As, week after week, I heard some great speakers, read lots of books, heard some not so good speakers and read some less than good books, mysterious things started happening within me. I started to become a different person and things awakened in me.

So here's the secret: We need to immerse ourselves in inspiration to be inspired.

Most of us don't grow up being immersed in inspiration. We need to expose ourselves to the gifts, talents, courage, dreams and love of other people to awaken the inspiration within us. Most of the messages we receive overtly through the media and subtly each day through the people around us are of lack, scarcity, shortages, wars, deficits, battles, dishonesty and selfishness. We receive fewer messages about love, inspiration, joy, beauty, creativity and forgiveness. If we listen to radio, watch TV and read newspapers, we are likely to have received vastly more negative than positive messages about life by the time we reach adulthood. We will also have received many more negative messages about ourselves than positive. By the time we reach adulthood, we have been given around 225,000 negative messages about ourselves and about 25,000 positive messages about ourselves—a ratio of 9:1. Too few of us receive messages about how inspiring we are, how powerful we can be and creative we are. But these qualities remain within us, often dormant because they haven't been affirmed and recognised by us and those around us.

Secret number 4

Keeping ourselves inspired is our responsibility

Action springs not from thought but from a readiness for responsibility.
Dietrich Bonhoeffer

When I worked in the corporate world, I used to think it was my boss's job to keep me motivated and inspired and, in my judgement, he didn't do a very good job. I realise now that it never was his job but I was reluctant to take responsibility for myself. Too often I gave my responsibility away to others through blame and apathy but I ended up living an unfulfilled and uninspired life.

Most people think that inspiration is an occasional thing that may or may not happen and that the Muse is capricious and unpredictable. Inspired people know that whatever the circumstances of their lives, inspiration is always a choice we can make. It's not that we can make it happen, it's that we can make ourselves receptive to *it*. I love the image of inspiration that Julia Cameron paints in her wonderful book *The Artists Way*. She sees inspiration like a radio frequency which is always being broadcast but *we* may not be tuned into *it*. BBC Radio 4 is always being broadcast even if we don't have our radios switched on. The same is true of inspiration; just because we don't experience it, doesn't mean it's not there, our job is to tune *ourselves* into *its* frequency.

We can't force ourselves to be inspired, we can't control inspiration, which is why many people have trouble with it. It is a mystery but a mystery we can build our lives on. We can make ourselves receptive to it. We do this by surrounding ourselves with inspiration but also by the choice to keep turning up to inspiration and creativity, however resistant we may feel. Our job is to put the welcome mat out for inspiration.

So here's the secret: It's our responsibility to keep ourselves aligned to inspiration.

Inspired people take the mystery of inspiration as a given; this doesn't mean they don't appreciate it or that they abuse it but they know their job is to be a conduit, a portal in time, opening themselves to continual inspiration and then mastering the craft of their taking ideas and moving through their resistance to turn those ideas into songs, plays, books, articles, software programmes, TV documentaries or whatever their craft is. Inspired people simply have no doubt about the ongoing and continual presence of inspiration; they know the job is to be the in-between—the channel between the divine and the time-bound.

Secret number 5

Inspiration is a choice not a chance

As we grow wiser, we become aware that the important forks in the road are usually not about choices that will show up on any public record; they are decisions and struggles to do with choosing love or fear; anger or forgiveness; pride or humility. They are soul-shaping choices.
Jean Shinoda Bolen

This is one of the biggest secrets that inspired people know. Uninspired people say to themselves, 'When I feel really motivated and inspired, I'll turn up and do my work.' Inspired people know that when they turn up and start doing their work, however they were feeling before, they start getting inspiration and the ideas begin to flow. Uninspired people don't know that often we have to cross a threshold to initiate the flow of inspiration.

When asked if he wrote on schedule or only when struck by inspiration, the writer Somerset Maugham replied, 'I write only when inspiration strikes. Fortunately it strikes every morning at nine o'clock sharp.' He knew that by choosing to turn up to inspiration, it turned up to him. Don't wait for inspiration because inspiration is waiting for you. We often have no idea of the power triggered by the simple and mundane act of sitting down and opening our pads or putting our hands on the keyboard. It's as if, by turning up, the Muse sets her watch to ours and the inspiration arrives when, *but not until*, we do. This is what uninspired people don't know; they are perpetually waiting, not understanding that the 'On!' switch is actually in their own hands.

So here's the secret: Inspiration turns up when we do and when we choose it.

I recently went to a talk by the children's writer Philip Pullman at the National Theatre in London. He was talking about the staging of his trilogy *His Dark Materials* as a three-part play at the National and answered a few questions. Someone asked him, 'Where does your inspiration come from?' I was dying to hear his response but felt disappointed when he explained, 'I don't know where inspiration comes *from*,' but he then continued and said, 'but I know it goes *to* my desk and if I am not there to receive it, it goes away again.' He knew the secret of inspiration—keep turning up and the Muse will meet you, like a regular blind date. Sometimes it takes what seems like a leap of faith to get inspiration going.

Secret number 6

Inspiration is a practical force in our lives

Inspiration is when our own soul shifts from being an abstract concept to an actual experience.
Barbara Winter, author of *Making a Living Without A Job*

Following inspiration is very practical; it is a force reliable enough and consistent enough on which to build a business and life. After 20 years spent as a well-paid nurse in the NHS, Jennifer Percival found herself newly divorced with a young son and a huge mortgage. She had every reason to talk herself into *not* changing, she could rationalise all the reasons why she *shouldn't* follow her inspiration. Yet she knew she had outgrown her job in nursing and wanted to find bigger ways to pursue her passion for communication and helping people change their lives.

After coming on one of my courses, she told me, 'I realised that I needed to change track. Money was at the root of all my fears and my negative thoughts blocked my creative energy. I had stopped trusting that the world was a place that could support my dreams. After doing the exercises I realised that all I needed was more confidence. I knew I was an excellent communicator and teacher. What I had to do was trust that my passion could produce enough income to support me and my son.' So she was inspired to begin writing articles and train as a counsellor whilst still working as nurse which then allowed her to cut her hours down to three days a week and start her own practice and business. Once she became more established, she moved into her own business full time.

She confided in me, 'I don't have a formal business plan, instead I follow my heart and my own inspiration. I found the most exciting thing has been waking up in the morning bursting with ideas, rushing into work and being able to put them into practice.' She is not a *flakey* person but an intensely practical State Registered Nurse, running her own business that now turns over more than £140,000 a year and has become the UK's Number One smoking cessation trainer. She now employs three other trainers to deliver her work to health promotion units throughout the UK and is now personally invited to present to nursing organisations internationally. She went on to explain, 'Creativity had not been part of my working life before. My policy since then is to follow my inspirations each and every day. I have learnt to trust the process of creation and know that somehow it always works out just right. New and exciting opportunities open up each week. If I have an idea I tell people about it. Many of these 'ideas' come back as offers of work.'

So here's the secret: We can bank on inspiration, literally!

Amazing things happen when we follow our inspired dreams but *not until we do*; we have to commit, as Jennifer did. Her next project is a book which she has published herself distilling the ideas that she teaches in her seminars. She continues to be amazed at how she finds that, as she follows through on one inspired idea, the next one is waiting; and her inspired ideas never run out. Jennifer has literally built her successful business on inspiration and following through on inspiration and has discovered the wonderful truth that *we don't do inspiration, it does us*. When we are truly inspired we will be shown the next step and, as we follow through, we are shown the next and the next. As she has responded to her own inner calling, she has developed the skills and abilities she needs and has expanded as she goes.

Secret number 7

Inspired people know that isolation kills inspiration

Isolation is the dreamkiller, not your attitude. No amount of positive thinking can replace information, encouragement and accountability. You need input and support from other people. They'll tell you things you need to know, encourage and believe in you and keep you moving toward your dream.
Barbara Sher, author of *Wishcraft*

Inspired people know that they need to break their isolation and join with other people. They know it is much harder to be inspired on their own and almost impossible to maintain that inspiration in a vacuum. It's been said that the quality of our lives is determined by the people with whom we associate and nowhere is that truer than around inspiration. Simply being in the presence of inspiration affirms us and lifts us up and we do that for others too; and a beautiful synergy emerges.

We need some kind of community of inspiration. It used to be that community was based on geography; we could only feel community with those to whom we lived close. Today is really the first time in history where we can create community based on consciousness and not on geography. We may feel more kinship with someone on the other side of the world than our next door neighbour or family of origin. Indeed, as Richard Bach, author of *Illusions,* expressed so beautifully, 'The members of one's true family seldom grow up under the same roof.' Our *tribe* is likely to be based on shared values and attitudes rather than blood ties and postcodes.

Whilst we lament the breakdown of community based on geography, never has there been more opportunity to create community of consciousness. It's never been easier to find or create inspirational networks and communities. Community allows us to see others and be seen ourselves, to have our gifts and talents acknowledged, to feel connected and part of something larger than ourselves. We can feel that we belong somewhere. People make us accountable, they want to know if we followed through on our dreams and what happened so they can support us, learn from us and be inspired by us.

So here's the secret: Inspired people choose to break their isolation and connect with others; they find or create their *tribe*.

Secret number 8

Inspired people see and create opportunity

Inspiration grows when you focus on solutions and opportunities, not problems and circumstances.
Barbara Winter, author of *Making a Living Without A Job*

Inspiration opens our eyes and raises our sights. Instead of just complaining and moaning about the world, inspiration calls us to be part of the transformation of the world. It calls us to put into the world what we see to be missing. We realise that every problem we see is an opportunity in disguise and the more we seize opportunities, the more they multiply. We don't do this by fighting against what we don't want but by creating what we truly *do* want, by helping a new world to be born through the love, kindness, intelligence and creativity within us. We don't expect other people to do it—and we love it when they do—but we are willing to take the first steps ourselves.

The world *is* full of unmet human needs and unfulfilled human aspirations but inspired people see this is as an opportunity to serve their fellow human beings. They also know that they have talents and gifts that could help. Who do you feel most called to help? How would you like to be helping them? One of the reasons why so many people become entrepreneurs is that one's own business offers unlimited opportunities to make a positive difference in the lives of others.

Often what inspired people feel called to be or do doesn't exist but they don't let that put them off. Often there isn't a demand for what we want to do before we do it but, once we do it, people are attracted to what we do. People often don't know what they want until they see it. People weren't queuing up for the Beatles before they started performing. Picasso didn't have a waiting list for paintings before he picked up a brush. I didn't receive letters and telephone calls saying, 'Please invent a concept and book called *The Work We Were*

Born To Do.' It's not until we share an idea, gift or talent that other people can resonate with it.

So here's the secret: Inspired people know that they create opportunity as they reveal their gifts and talents to the world.

Section two:
Nurturing our inspired ideas

Inspired ideas are centres of consciousness, often calling us to grow, learn and develop beyond what we think are our capabilities.

Secret number 9

Inspired people know that their great ideas often come in a size that seems too big

We never become truly spiritual by sitting down and wishing to become so. You must undertake something so great that you cannot accomplish it unaided.
Philip Brooks

Our inspired ideas often come in a size too big for us and, sometimes, so big that we don't recognise them at first, assuming they are either fantasies or great ideas but for someone else. We need to develop a new kind of vision which involves recognising that inherent within our most inspired ideas is often a call to growth.

Dreams by definition are bold, daring and imaginative. We need the pull of inspiration that a big dream offers in order to draw us forward. We may be both thrilled and a little daunted. Dreams must be powerful enough to compel us forward and make us want to get out of bed each morning. We are shown a preview of coming attractions but not cruelly shown something that we can never attain. We are shown what we are in our hearts already but what we need to grow into. Within inspiration is an invitation to grow and grow and grow but the gap between who we are now and who we are called to become can seem too large. We may need to learn new skills, grow in self-belief and confidence, develop emotional maturity and conquer our fears; but that *is* the spiritual path.

I remember sitting at my desk in Holborn in London in the late 1980's, when I was still in computer sales. Although I was well paid, I was increasingly unhappy and unfulfilled and came to the conclusion that I had not been put on this planet to sell computers to Japanese banks in the city of London. As you probably experience, often knowing what we *don't* want is the easier bit; we find knowing what we truly *do* want is the harder part. So I began to ask myself those bigger questions, like *why am I here?* And *what would really inspire me?* As I asked the questions, I began to receive answers; 'You are here to inspire people, to be creative, to teach and write.' At that time I couldn't even inspire myself, let alone anyone else, and thought the answers were great but not for me. I guessed I must have been receiving someone else's mail by mistake. I didn't recognise my own destiny because I was afraid. I was being invited to change but the fear this stimulated in me was huge, so I fought this sense of inspiration for a couple of years until it began to dawn on me that I was being shown my own way forward. I was being invited to grow.

So here's the secret: Our inspired ideas often come in a size too big for us so that we can grow into them.

Being inspired is signing up for an adventure in growth, becoming more than we thought we were. We must recognise that growth is an hourly, daily, weekly and monthly journey. It's a step-by-step process and the only way to become who we will be is to accept who we are and learn and grow a little every day. And the journey is as important as the arrival, as arrival becomes a daily process too.

Secret number 10

We apprentice ourselves to inspiration

If people knew how hard I worked to get my mastery, it wouldn't seem so wonderful after all.
Michelangelo

There was a TV programme about *Cirque du Soleil*, the Canadian circus group, documenting the creation of one of their new shows. One of the things I have always loved about *Cirque* is what seems to be their creativity and effortless artistry, making impossible things seem both possible and easy. The programme showed them starting rehearsals and I was quite shocked—they were awful! They were dropping each other, arguing and missing the mark regularly. And then it began to dawn on me that the superb performances I have the pleasure of witnessing in their live shows were only possible because the performers had been willing to be bad to start with. They are on a continual journey of arrival. Although the *Cirque* artists were all individually competent, in this new show as a team they weren't yet competent. This is something *wannabe* creative artists don't or won't understand. Those they admire and revere have been willing to serve, and will continually serve, an apprenticeship.

As adults we find it hard to be beginners; we want to be immediately competent, we are unwilling to look a little silly to begin with. But we are always still learning and discovering new levels of mastery, we are developing our craft. At the point when Barbara and I were inspired by the idea of Dreambuilders Community in May 2003, between us we had a combined entrepreneurial experience of nearly 50 years, yet we looked at each other and said, 'We feel like we're back at the beginning.' We were both inspired and daunted.

So here's the secret: Some things take a few moments to learn and a lifetime to master.

Please don't confuse this with the protestant work ethic that says *anything valuable is only ever achieved through hard work, struggle and sacrifice.* There is a very different quality to the energy involved in needless struggle to try and make oneself a more noble person and the willing energy expended in achieving mastery of our craft. Don't make it hard for the sake of it. Ease, grace and miracles are also there for us and we can open ourselves to them in each moment. Our inspiration shapes and moulds us into the person we were destined to be and sometimes the apprenticeship takes us through challenges, seeming failures, vulnerabilities and disappointments, as well as success. With awareness, all these things positively shape us. Everything can make us wiser.

Secret number 11

Inspired people build self-confidence as they go

I have never begun any important venture for which I felt adequately prepared.
Sheldon Kopp, author of *If You Meet the Buddha on the Road, Kill Him*

One form of resistance is *waiting*, usually until we feel more confident before we start a project or until we feel better about ourselves or our self-esteem improves. Self-belief and self-confidence have always been weak areas for me, so I used to go on workshops, do prayers and affirmations and get coached and counselled to try and feel better about myself. It helped a bit but those feelings never went away. I realised I was waiting until I had sorted out of all my issues before I started on my dreams and creative projects. This is what I learned and it's my one great tip for building confidence: *Be honest about what you'd be doing if you already had self-belief and start doing it, even in tiny ways, taking action and move through fear and resistance.*

Taking action is one of the most powerful ways of busting through fear and resistance and building confidence on the journey. This is the path of courage—growing through action, acting in the face of fear and doubt and with whatever self-confidence we have in this moment. We have so much more power, so many more resources inside us, which we only discover by being involved with and engaged in life. Thomas Merton, the monk and spiritual writer, once said, 'Do it trembling if you must but do it!' Sometimes it takes every ounce of courage and self-belief to take even a tiny step but do it anyway. Inaction breeds doubt and fear while action breeds confidence and courage. If we want to conquer fear, we won't do it sitting at home and thinking about it but by going out and taking focused action. Fearbusting and confidence building are actually the same thing—as we take action in the face of fear, confidence grows as we do it. Often we don't know what we are capable of until we are given, or we create, the opportunity.

So here's the secret: Confidence turns up as and when we do, it meets us at the point of action. Taking action is the quickest way to build confidence.

Secret number 12

Inspired people know that life is a series of graduations

As you grow, your consciousness develops. As your consciousness grows, you attract more prosperity to you....You must be willing to do the personal development necessary to become the person who is trusted and blessed with great prosperity.
Randy Gage, author of *The 37 Secrets about Prosperity*

Many people are unaware of, or are unwilling to invest in, the gradual and alchemical process of growth. They want to be *there* already but the problem is that, even if they get there, they'll have trouble staying there. Inspired people know that there are no shortcuts to success; if we try to build something on shaky foundations it won't be stable and secure and could even collapse. Just like a tree has deep and strong roots in the earth in order to grow tall, we need to have strong roots in *the invisible earth of our consciousness*. As *we* grow within ourselves, our confidence, wealth, opportunity, influence and territory will grow.

Inspired people know that as they graduate to a new level of consciousness, they start manifesting at that new level. We understand that success isn't something to pursue but something we naturally attract through the person we've become; or, more precisely, it's about who we reveal ourselves to be. We've always been our spiritual selves, we've just hidden it from the world and even from ourselves.

So here's the secret: Be willing to grow, invest in yourself and your own consciousness, knowing that as you do every good thing is waiting for you.

When we grow and it's time to graduate, we don't then join a long queue while a bunch of cosmic bureaucrats figure out what to do with us next. The universe is standing and waiting on tiptoes *for us* to graduate, actively participating in our growth and it has our next opportunities all lined up and ready to go. We can often feel that in advance; even though we don't know what the next assignment will be, we feel the anticipation of it and we have faith in that process.

Secret number 13

Inspired ideas have a life of their own

The work will teach you how to do it.
Estonian Proverb

Inspired people know that their great ideas have *lives in potential* encoded within them, destinies waiting to unfold. The ideas have their own evolutionary paths waiting to be revealed, just as a sunflower seed is destined to become a sapling, a beautiful big plant, a beautiful flower that when it dies bestows hundreds of seeds to repeat and continue the process. Inspiration wants to unfold *us*; when we become partners with our inspired ideas, a mutual intimacy develops between our inner and outer lives. But inspired people don't worry about *how to* too soon, they don't try and solve problems they don't have yet. They know they will learn what they need to as they need to.

I have experienced this in my life in many ways, one of the most significant being the way that *The Work We Were Born To Do* has evolved over the years. I had already been running some events around work and inspiration when, one day in 1994, the words *The Work We Were Born To Do* came into my mind. I knew this had at least two strands to it; it was what I was discovering for myself and it was what I wanted to help others discover. I asked myself 'What shall I do with this idea?' and the first idea was to give a talk in London which I prepared and delivered; it went well and created some invitations to give the talk elsewhere too. Then I felt inspired to turn it to a day workshop, so I did that and it went well. Then I felt inspired to create some quotation cards which I did and still use them to this day.

So here's the secret: Inspired people know and recognise the power and inner life of a great idea.

Then I felt the urge to create a tape of my talks which was quite a struggle. Every time I gave a talk and recorded it, I decided it wasn't good enough to make into a tape. So that took a couple of years to get beyond my perfectionism and my fear to create a tape which eventually sold a thousand copies. Like most people, I hoped that one day I might write a book and by now I was in my late thirties, so I decided it was time to discover whether this was an inspired idea waiting to happen or a fantasy. So I bought a laptop computer and started to formulate and expand ideas that might become a book. After a year or so I showed my ideas to publishers and one of them offered me a contract. I was terrified—could I write a whole book? Was I up to it? But I checked out with my soul and received a resounding 'Yes! It's one of the reasons you are here!' So I signed the contract and immediately felt at peace. I wrote solidly for three months and, when the book came out in 1999, it started creating more and more connections, opening doors to speak around the UK, Europe, USA and South Africa.

Last month I travelled to speak in six different countries, all because of that one idea; *The Work We Were Born To Do*. It's an idea that has had a major impact on my life and the lives of thousands of other people. I am sure that single idea will continue to unfold for the rest of my life and it will grow and mature, as well as me having tons more ideas every day! Sometimes we don't need more ideas, we simply need to evolve the ideas we already have. We don't have to figure out all the details, they have lives of their own and, to some extent, we are the midwives of the ideas, giving birth to them and ourselves at the same time. Then we become their parents, caring for them and watching them grow up into what they are destined to be. They will teach us, if we let them, if we enter into a strong relationship with them and let them lead the way. The writer Douglas Adams put it this way; 'I may not have gone where I intended to go but I think I have ended up where I intended to be.'

Secret number 14

Inspiration is an evolutionary force in our lives

*I am permanently pregnant with the next play ... Each time I give birth
to a play, I am impregnated with the idea for the next.*
Alan Ayckborne, playwright, after writing his 66th play

When we say yes to inspiration, we have hooked ourselves up to
a greater force than ourselves. Inspiration doesn't leave us as it
found us, it transforms and evolves us to become different people.
After my first book *The Work We Were Born To Do* came out in 1999,
I had a regular flow of people who would ask me questions like, 'I
have an idea for a book. How should I start writing? Do I have to write
the whole thing before I show a publisher? Do I need an agent? What
is a publishing proposal and what do I need to put in it?' After a year
or so of answering these questions individually, I suddenly had a flash
of inspiration: *why don't we organise an event where we could answer
these questions for lots of people, all at the same time?* I ran this idea
past Steve Nobel, who is a director of Alternatives in St. James's in
Piccadilly, and out of our conversation an event called *Publish Your
Book* was born. We got another author, a publishing consultant and an
agent all to give their perspectives on what to do and many people have
now moved forward with their creativity; some have become
published authors. The first event had 150 people attend it and sold out
three weeks beforehand; we have run it five times since and I have also
run this seminar in three other countries on my own.

**So here's the secret: We'll always be pregnant with the next idea
when we follow through on the current one.**

A few years ago, before I had written my own book, if someone had
said to me that one day I was going to help writers unleash their
creativity and help them take their ideas to the market place, I would
have been incredulous and probably laughed at them. I was struggling
to do that for myself; I needed to grow a lot more before I could that.
But that is the way inspiration works—it unfolds our path one step at

a time, taking us to places that we can't even anticipate. Only when I followed through on the first inspiration to start writing and then approach a publisher and then become published was I finally in a place where it occurred to me to start helping others.

Too often we want to know how the whole future is going to look when we are called simply to take the next step, at which time the step afterwards will be revealed. We discover that when we align ourselves with inspiration, we apprentice ourselves to a force and intelligence much greater than our own personalities. This power sees a bigger picture than we do, sees that our gifts and talents can best be utilised and continually nudges forward, urging us to grow. It also helps co-ordinate the connections we need to succeed.

As we evolve we also mature and, like a fine wine, our souls mature. Oak trees do not produce acorns until they are fifty years of age or older and, as we grow in wisdom and maturity, our work and creativity will mature too.

Secret number 15

Inspired people know where they get their best ideas

It's important to understand that taking a short time-out to refuel and refresh doesn't mean that you are goofing off. When you take a break, your brain doesn't shut off. The ideas that you have been considering shift to a 'back burner' where they incubate. The problems you've been working on make an unconscious shift from the left (logical) to the right (creative) brain. And then, boom! When you least expect it, the lightning strikes.'
Robert J. Kriegel author of *How to Succeed in Business Without Working So Damn Hard: Rethinking the Rules, Reinventing the Game*

Our inspired ideas are our best ideas and we need to know what supports us to generate inspired ideas. I was chatting with June, a manager in an NHS trust, during a course I was running on inspiration and she confided in me, 'I have a report to prepare on new strategies for service delivery. I sit at my desk trying to come up with ideas and nothing happens. I know if I went for a walk with my dog along the cliff tops I would get all the ideas I need but I feel guilty about leaving my desk. I am supposed to be seen to be working hard.' June was half way there—she knew how she generated her best ideas but hadn't given herself permission to go to that place.

So here's the secret: Inspired people know how and where to get their best ideas and go there regularly.

Do you know where you get your best ideas? Barbara Winter has a theory—she believes that ideas are repelled by cubicles and boring offices. She believes they are very rarely about to penetrate into them. We need open space, both inner and outer; we need to take the pressure off ourselves for the magic to happen. It's really important that we know the people, places, ideas and stories that help trigger our best ideas. I know that many of my best ideas come to me after a (short) workout at my gym when I am sitting in the sauna and steam room. I know that when I spend time with Barbara I always come away with lots of great ideas. I know that when I read autobiographies of entrepreneurs I get lots of ideas, as I do at seminars, in my coaching sessions and at conferences.

What do you do when you get great ideas? I suggest capturing them; write them down and they will feel honoured and you are putting the welcome mat out for more. Be slow to dismiss them and adopt a curiosity about them. *How could that work? How could I adapt that idea? What do I like about that idea?* Get your creative juices going and be open. Often we need someone outside us to stimulate and even challenge us with new ideas. Other people don't have the emotional attachment we do, the limiting beliefs we do, they aren't caught in our way of thinking. Search the internet and you'll find hundreds of techniques for generating ideas.

Section three:
Understanding resistance

Resistance is our own inner enemy, the force within us that tries to squash our inspiration. The more important an idea is to us, the more likely we are to resist it.

Secret number 16

Inspired people acquaint themselves with the force of resistance

Most of us have two lives. The life we live and the unlived life within us. Between the two stands Resistance.
Steven Pressfield, author of *The War of Art*

Have you ever had an idea for a business enterprise and not followed through? Or an idea for a book that is still unwritten? Or a great creative project that you've never got off the drawing board? If you say yes to any of those, you know resistance. Resistance kicks in when we are thinking about starting, when we've started and all along the journey; we need to learn to live with it and overcome it every day. Resistance is our own inner enemy that stops us being creative. It's the emotional and psychological force that stops writers writing, stops entrepreneurs starting businesses, stops talented people succeeding.

The most important thing to understand about resistance is that it is *impersonal*. There is nothing wrong with *you* because you resist, it's not special to you. It's not a character flaw, a personal defect or a family trait; it's simply part of the territory of being human. Resistance shows up in so many ways—procrastination, rationalisation, excuses, regular emotional drama, self-sabotage, excess busyness and lack of time, being a perfectionist and control freak, addictions. Resistance is less about the activity itself and more about the purpose we give the activity. Of course the windows need to be kept clean but if we have a spotless home and our book remains unstarted, that's resistance.

It's crucial that we understand resistance and become aware of our particular ways of resisting because, if we don't, it will beat us and we won't even have seen it coming. Although I am not a rugby player, I used to experience resistance like this; I would have a great idea and get inspired and, like a rugby player, I'd start running with the ball towards the line to score a try. Then suddenly out of nowhere I'd be on the floor scrabbling around in the mud. Some force I didn't even see coming whacked me and I would be lying dazed and confused and limp off the pitch wondering what was wrong with me. That is how unconscious resistance can seem; an inner force that suddenly erupts from within our own minds, creating an invisible wall that we can't get beyond. Some people call that our shadow side.

So here's the secret: Inspired people become aware of resistance and learn how to handle it and move through it.

Secret number 17

Inspired people know how powerful resistance can be

Thousands of people have talent. I might as well congratulate you for having eyes in your head. The one and only thing that counts is: do you have staying power?
Noel Coward, actor and playwright

Inspired people don't doubt they have talent and they know that inspiration and great ideas will never be in short supply. They can take that for granted. They recognise that their success is partly created by their talents but will also be determined by their capacity to recognise and move through their own resistance.

As powerful as is our souls' longing for inspiration, resistance seems to have an equal and opposite power to stop us from realising our potential. It is literally as if the forces of Heaven and the forces of Hell are played out within us. Without awareness, resistance can seem even more powerful; whilst with an awareness and understanding of resistance, we can conquer resistance. Our powers of inspiration and creativity are greater but we need awareness and skill to win over resistance. We need to understand that most of the times when we become inspired and are drawn to creative expression within minutes, days or months, we are also likely to experience resistance. This is not personal, not a character defect, not something that is special to you alone, it is simply the territory of being human. Indeed, the more important an idea, venture or endeavour to our soul's evolution *the more likely we are to experience resistance.* So here's the trick: the more we become aware of what we are resisting, the more we can use this as a pointer and homing beacon—pointing us *at* our North Star.

So here's the secret: Inspired people know that their success is a combination of talent and the ability to move through resistance.

Each of us has a genius, a difference we promised to make, a dream we promised to fulfil. Each of us has the seat of the soul, a sacred place within us from which we can share our unique gifts. Basically, resistance is the process by which we imprison our own creativity; it is the way we stop ourselves becoming who we were born to be, discovering and giving our gifts, being creative and making the contribution we promised to make to Life.

Secret number 18

Inspired people understand the positive aspect of resistance

All suffering comes from violation of intuition.
Florence Scovel-Shinn, author of *The Secret Door to Success*

Inspired people learn that resistance does actually have two positive aspects. Firstly, when we understand the process of resistance, we know that what we are most resisting is usually the place we are most called to go creatively. It's just fear trying to stop us. This resistance points us *at* our essence.

Secondly we sometimes resist for the right reasons, simply because something *isn't* right for us. At the end of one of my trips to South Africa my colleague Richard asked me to meet Jan, a businessman who wanted to work with us. Richard said the two of them had met four times already and Jan was pushing Richard to go ahead on a couple of projects but he'd not gone ahead so far. We met at Johannesburg zoo and spent an hour walking around and, as Richard drove me to the airport to come home, I said, 'You were right not to go ahead with Jan. I don't think he's on our wavelength and that we'd be able to retain the integrity of what we are doing with him. He seems more interested in the money.' Richard looked incredibly relieved and explained that he had felt similarly but tried to override his instincts because it made logical sense to work with Jan.

So here's the secret: Sometimes what seems like resistance is actually our intuition quietly screaming 'Don't go there, it would be a mistake.'

This resistance warns us that we are moving *away* from our essence. We are trained to value logic over intuition, so we often try to make our feelings fit the facts rather than trust our intuition. Most of us know the pain we cause ourselves when we override our instincts and we know the fruits of following them.

Of course, the million pound questions are, 'How do we discern which resistance we are dealing with? Are we avoiding from fear or avoiding through positive intuition?' This partly comes from experience, knowing and trusting ourselves, and here is a great way I use to discern; I ask myself 'If I wasn't feeling afraid, would I want to do this?' With Jan, the answer was a clear, 'No!' I just didn't want to work with him, I felt no affinity with him. If we recognise that if it weren't for fear, we'd want to go ahead, then we know that we are dealing with the fear aspect of resistance. Be brutally honest with yourself, though; don't resist out of fear and then rationalise it away as '*it wasn't right for me.*' You may fool others but your self esteem will suffer badly. You can't fool yourself.

Secret number 19

Inspired people recognise their master fear

The Mother of all fears is so close to us that even when we verbalise it we don't believe it: The fear that we will succeed.
Steven Pressfield, author of *The War of Art*

We are all afraid of something or another, it's the ground of being human. We are afraid of failing, of looking stupid, poverty and insolvency, of making lousy choices that we can't undo and are stuck with and we have to come grovelling back to where we started. We are afraid of disappointing others who have sacrificed for us, of not making the most of the training and education we had, we are afraid of starting again once we've invested in one direction. We are afraid of humiliation, death or being insane to follow a silly idea that won't go away.

These fears are enough to stop most people being inspired, creative and following their hearts and most people are stopped by these fears. But whilst these fears are real, inspired people know that they are actually a distraction, a smoke screen for the master fear—fear of success. As Marianne Williamson tells us, 'Our deepest fear is not that we are inadequate. Our deepest fear is that we are powerful beyond measure. You are a child of God.' It's the good stuff we are afraid of; we are afraid of the light. We are afraid to discover that we are more than we think we are, more than our teachers, family and friends think we are. We are afraid that we do have the power, talent, gifts and abilities that our still small voice tells us we have. We are afraid our dreams are not fantasies but realities in embryo. We are afraid of the magnificence and beauty we feel in our heart. We are afraid that we can steer our ships, give up our excuses and find our own promised lands. How could we be that lovely, that open, and survive in the world? We try to convince ourselves that we should be normal and ordinary.

Why are we so afraid of the good stuff, our own power and greatness? We are afraid to be different, to be extraordinary, to stand out, to shine, to think well of ourselves. We fear that we'd become estranged from the people we know, love, care for and respect—in essence, we fear we'd lose love, approval and acceptance. We might be judged harshly, lose our friends and family. They'll no longer know us or recognise us. We may not even recognise ourselves anymore. We'll end up afraid out there all alone.

So here's the secret: Inspired people are willing to recognise and give up their fear of success.

As we begin to embrace our greatness, some of our fears do materialise. We do lose a few friends; some people will feel betrayed and relate to us less. But instead of finding ourselves alone, we discover new friends who see, encourage, celebrate and support us. Instead of the fear that controls the majority of people, we find ourselves supported by an invisible force of wisdom, ideas and inspiration that never runs out. We stand on the ground of consciousness. We recognise that life is set up to support and celebrate our power, creativity and prosperity. And most importantly we recognise that only we, by our thinking and attitudes, are depriving ourselves of anything. We recognise that there is nothing outside of ourselves. We know what the mystic poet, Rumi, told us, 'The source is within you and this whole cosmos is springing up from it.'

Secret number 20

The resistance never goes away—get used to it!

We are facing dragons too. Fire-breathing griffins of the soul, whom we must outfight and outwit to reach the treasure of our self-in-potential and to release the maiden who is God's plan and destiny for ourselves and the answer to why we were put on this planet.
Steven Pressfield, author of *The War of Art*

I felt such triumph having completed the creative process of writing my first book; and then enormous pleasure in getting it published and even greater triumph that people seemed to like it! I was proud of having broken through so much of my own resistance to do it. I thought I was home and dry and beyond resistance.

Wrong! Several publishers were now interested in me writing further books and I had some meetings. Then I began to notice what seemed like a very rational voice in my head saying to me, 'You know what Nick? You've done so well with your first book with lots of critical acclaim and great fulfilment. How would you feel if your next books weren't so good and weren't so well received? You'd be seen as a one-hit wonder and written off. Why not stick at writing one book, then people will always think you are capable of more but you don't actually have to risk doing more and you remove the possibility of ever looking stupid.' It seemed to make sense and I nearly fell for it. Then I realised it was resistance and self-sabotage. My soul was telling me that I had barely got warmed up with my creativity and there was plenty more where that had come from. But that voice of self-undermining didn't go away and I actually found *Unconditional Success* a lot harder to write than my first book, mainly because of resistance, that voice telling me I might fail, not because of any shortage of ideas.

So here's the secret: Inspired people become experts on spotting and moving through their resistance and don't allow it to stop them.

We truly are in a battle with ourselves when it comes to inspiration and creativity and we must learn that, as we move the creative bar higher, so resistance will bring out bigger guns. What makes successfully creative people successful is as much about their ability to recognise and conquer their own resistance, to win the battle over their own negativity and self-doubting, as is it about their ability. Does a lot of talent go unfulfilled because of resistance? Of course; I would suggest that the majority of talent goes unexpressed. Too often we are afraid to show our talents because of the voices of resistance; but then we all lose. We don't experience the joy of expressing and sharing our gifts and the world loses the blessings that our gifts bring. You have talents and gifts inside you. Please don't hold them back, we need them to brighten our world.

Secret number 21

Inspired people act in the face of fears, not the absence of fears

When we conceive of an enterprise and commit to it in the face of our fears, something wonderful happens. A crack appears in the membrane. Like the first craze when a chick pecks at the inside of its shell. Angel midwives congregate around us; they assist as we give birth to ourselves, to that person we were born to be, to the one whose destiny was encoded in our soul, our daemon, our genius. When we make a beginning, we get out of our own way and allow the angels to come in and do their job.
Steven Pressfield, author of *The War of Art*

Most people rob themselves of inspiration because they are waiting for the fear and resistance to subside before they act. Good luck! Truly inspired and creative people know that a resistance-free day is a rare day. That doesn't mean that every day we have to be brought to our knees by doubt or engage in emotional drama; but it does mean that every day we are likely to meet some opposing force to our dreams and inspiration. An amateur believes that the fear must subside before doing the work; a professional knows that we dissolve our fears *by* doing our work. Fear dissolves by being in the flow but not while we are standing on the riverbank. Knowing this, we choose to act anyway and that activates something magical. When we act anyway, new ideas come through as we can hear the angels speaking to us and it makes *them* happy and *us* happy. It makes God happy.

So here's the secret: Magic happens when we consistently act in the face of fears.

This doesn't just happen once but can happen over and over again. The most important thing about being creative is simply to do our work every day. By keeping inspiration flowing we keep the membrane between the worlds thin, we keep ourselves moving through our own resistance. The river can carry us. This so important because, as we commit each to do our work, something mysterious continues to happen. A process is set into motion by which, inevitably and infallibly, heaven comes to our aid. We become attractive, like a magnetised iron rod that attracts iron filings. The Muse smiles on our commitment and bestows blessings upon us. Unseen forces enlist in our cause; serendipity reinforces our sense of purpose and we find ourselves in a flow of ideas, creativity and confirming feedback that simply wouldn't have occurred if we hadn't acted.

In what ways could you be acting in the face of resistance and fear today—and tomorrow?

Secret number 22

Inspired people are willing to develop emotional courage

Those who do not know how to weep with their whole heart don't know how to laugh either.
Golda Meir, former Prime Minister of Israel

A common misconception about being inspired is that it is just about being *up*. The more committed we become to being inspired, the greater the emotional darkness we will at times probably have to face, too, and we need to discover ways through. One of the pieces of the Buddha's wisdom was, 'Desire nothing, resist nothing.' We need to learn how to feel all our feelings but not get caught in them. There have been countless times when I have and still do weep with frustration and despair, feel disappointed, angry at God for life being so difficult that I want to give up. I am learning to get through those times more quickly than I did. I believe that creative and inspired people at times have to plumb the depths of their own darkness and face their difficult feelings and bring the light to those dark places. They do this over and again to make themselves safer and make the world safer for everyone. One of the greatest things we can learn is simply to feel our feelings, without blaming anyone else for them, without dumping them and without attacking others. Our goal is to transform our suffering so our heart is more open, we are more compassionate and more loving.

So here's the secret: Inspired people develop authentic vulnerability. They get to accept and make friends with all their emotions, using them to open their hearts, rather than harden them.

I remember hearing Elizabeth Kubler Ross, psychiatrist and prolific author, say that she believed that there was an inner Hitler in all of us. That didn't mean that all of us were evil; she meant that everything we judge is a fragment of ourselves. Inspired and courageous people pick up a mirror and look at themselves before they point their finger and judge. They have the courage to accept and integrate *all* aspects of themselves, even the unpleasant ones.

Section four:
Creative action and expression

Inspiration calls us to creative action and to make our own souls visible in the world.

Secret number 23

Inspiration makes us artists of the soul

Every day is an opportunity to be creative—the canvas is your mind, the brushes and colours are your thoughts and feelings, the panorama is your story, the complete picture is a work of art called, 'my life.' Be careful what you put on the canvas of your mind today—it matters.
Brahma Kumaris, spiritual foundation

The future is not some place we are going but one we are creating. The paths to it are not found but made and the activity of making them changes both the maker and the destination. The Latin root of the word inspiration is *in spire* meaning 'in-breath.' If the inspiration is the drawing in of spiritual breath, the out-breath is creativity. Inspiration is the precursor of creative expression and action. Inspiration wants us to become artists of the soul. Unfortunately, most of us have too narrow a definition of what an artist is. We think artists are particularly gifted and express that through media like painting, pottery, writing or dance. I think that anyone who becomes inspired is an artist and practically anything can become the canvas of our expression: our businesses, our families, our relationships, our shops, our communities, our work, our art, can all be the canvases onto which we paint our own souls. What are the canvases onto which you paint your creativity?

Our creativity can take at least two forms. Firstly, we can do *ordinary* things in creative and inspired ways, by infusing them with our unique energy, love and experience. Secondly, we can be creative by *bringing something into being*, a business, a painting, a child, a home or some other project. The more we become inspired, the greater the natural desire to express and embody outside of ourselves the divine and spiritual element we find within ourselves. The closer we grow to our inner light, the more we feel the natural urge to share what we find within us with others. We long for ways in which our creative energies can extend into the world whether through work, relationships or family. In essence, we want a way for our love to flow into the world.

So here's the secret: Inspired people know they will become more and more creative.

Secret number 24

Inspired people are drawn out of hiding

Shadow artists gravitate towards their rightful tribe but cannot yet claim their birthright ... they are hiding in the shadows, afraid to expose the dream to the light, fearful that it will disintegrate to the touch... Shadow artists often choose shadow careers—those close to the desired art, even parallel to it, but not the art itself.
Julia Cameron, author of *The Artists Way*

Too often we don't willingly answer the call of inspiration. We pretend we don't hear it or now is not the right time or somehow the Muse must have got the wrong person. Sometimes we have to be dragged kicking and screaming to our creativity. One of the roles that inspiration plays is to draw us out of hiding; it wants our gifts and talents fully owned, recognised and utilised, not denied or hidden away. Inspiration calls us fully to become all that we already are. Often we don't know we are hiding away our creativity, we are so used to doing it, we may have forgotten it was even there. Our hiding out can take several forms. We often end up in a supporting role, nurturing the creativity of others and helping them succeed—we could nurture the creativity of our children, our clients, our friends and colleagues. We may simply deny our own creativity and pretend we don't see it. We may even become a critic, often a fierce one, to cover up our own frustration. We may criticise others, and believe we can do better, but we never put that to the test.

When we were young we probably weren't seen and affirmed as being creative, so while our own creativity often shows itself by drawing us to the creative force field of others, we stay on the edge of our own creativity. This offers a degree of satisfaction but we will never be deeply fulfilled until we let our own creativity see the light of day. We may want to write a book and end up working for a publisher; we may aspire to direct a film and end up as a second production assistant; we may want to act but become an agent; we may want to design jewellery but work in a shop selling the jewellery others made. Close but not quite there.

In 1997 I realised that being a director of Alternatives had become a way of hiding out for me. There I was, promoting the spirituality and creativity of others while my own voice remained largely quiet. I had things to say, too, but I was afraid to say them, believing others would and could say them better than me. All shadow artists are actually afraid to put their creativity at the centre of their lives. We need to get honest and say, 'You know what, I am terrified. I don't know if I am that creative, if I have anything to really say, and don't know whether I can do it. But I am willing to find out.' Inspiration calls us to move beyond our fear to the full expression of our creativity. The poet David Whyte reminds us, 'Life is constantly orphaning us from our old homes but always into a much larger territory than we think we can inhabit to start with.' As the aphorism says, 'Sometimes even eagles need a push to leave their nest and fly.'

So here's the secret: Inspiration won't let us hide; it wants us to be seen fully and to exist fully.

Sometimes when we experience someone else's creativity expressed, we have a shock of recognition, a feeling of *How dare they be and do what I am so afraid to be and do?* Great creative expression can strike us with the shock of recognition, the wish *we* had expressed that. Our souls thrill at the reminder of what we all already know. We experience that mixture of inspiration and frustration and the recognition that we could be that too.

We can be very public but still hide. I recently saw the actor Hugh Grant on TV talking about his career. He explained on the Channel 4 chat show *Richard and Judy*, 'I am bored stiff with acting but it pays so well. I would love to write and direct.' But he hadn't written or directed; he was famously hiding out and in fear of being ridiculed in a new area of creativity. He stuck with the old and familiar areas. It was sad to see him looking so unhappy. When we hide, everyone loses; when we step into full expression, we all win. When we are full-out creative, we know that deepest joy for ourselves; our gifts touch the lives of others; we awaken inspiration and dreams in others.

Secret number 25

Inspired people become midwives

As the mother-to-be bears her child within her, so the artist or innovator contains her new life. No one can help her give birth. But neither does she need any help. The mother and the artist are both watched over by Heaven.
Steven Pressfield, author of *The War of Art*

When it comes to inspiration and inspired ideas, we need to recognise that we are vehicles, not originators. We don't create new life, we only bear it. That is not to diminish our role but to put it in its true perspective. That's why birth, inspiration and creativity are such humbling experiences. Our creativity comes out of us but not from us; it is where the divine and the human in us meet. We become divine agents. Artists who think they are the originators of their creativity are in for trouble but, when we know we can open ourselves up to becoming a channel, the continual birth process can happen through us.

When we serve heaven rather than the market, we align ourselves with the mysterious forces that power the universe and that seek, through us, to bring forward new life and new ideas. By serving the universe, we put ourselves in service of these forces. We know deep in our hearts we don't know a lot; we are being taught and inspired every day. We know we are divinely winging it, knowing that inspiration will keep showing up as we do. We know something is next, not usually what. We can't guess what inspiration is going to say but we can open ourselves to receive it. Each day we can ask ourselves, 'What do I feel growing inside me? What is seeking expression through me? How can I bring that forth?' We free ourselves of fear when we seek to be creative for its own sake and become less attached to what creativity can do for us, our standing and impressing others; in other words for our ego needs. The more we become a divine agent, the more we experience the sustenance that comes from the act of creation itself, rather than the impact it has on others. The more we do it for ourselves, the more we cut the ground from underneath resistance.

So here's the secret: Our jobs are to be earthly midwives birthing divine ideas.

This is a huge lesson for us to learn; how can we be inspired and creative in order to serve Life, not just satisfy the market. When we focus mainly on *the market* we become like a hack—only doing what we think will make us popular and earn us money.

Secret number 26

A powerful relationship with fear

It's been proven that the only effective way to deal with fear is to walk through it, through the pain that accompanies doing something you're afraid to do. It takes courage to fulfil your commitments, courage to stay on track, courage to follow your dreams, courage to reach your goals and courage to walk through your fear.
Francine Ward

When most people experience fear, they have one of two major conditioned responses; they see a stop sign, *Don't go there!* Or their defences are raised which includes attacking what they perceive as the source of their fear. In both cases their fears have them, fear determines their response to fear but either way they are disempowered. *A Course in Miracles* teaches us that 'Every decision is a choice between love and fear.' Inspired people become aware of their conditioned responses and realise that there is always a choice to fear. Whether we call that choice love, courage, trust, creativity or inspiration doesn't matter. Inspired and creative people know that another option is that *fear is a call to growth* and that knowing our fears and acting in the face of them, we become greater people.

So here's the secret: Often the places where we are afraid to go are the places where the greatest gifts are and are the places we are actually called to go.

Within fear is also its downfall. Fear wants to keep us small and, when we know that, we can look for the *bigness and the gifts* that the fear is trying to hide. So here is what inspired people know—by growing through our fears, we liberate ourselves from our fears. We discover through experience, not just as an idea, that there is a force greater than fear. Gradually, deep in our bones, we know that although fear seems the most powerful force on the planet, it isn't. Fears melt away in the light of courage, awareness and love but we can do this by facing our fears, not avoiding them.

So inspired people are on a path of developing greater levels of courage. Funnily enough, though, we need courage to face a fear but, once we've faced it, it no longer requires our courage. The power it had *over* us is now available *to* us; we transform its energy and integrate it into us. Our fear was our power repressed but it now becomes available as we acquire the strength of what we have overcome. We are on a path to become a pioneer of the future and cease being a prisoner of the past. We build self-confidence as the result of taking risks. Once we have successfully taken risks, we have learned through our experiences that we can count on ourselves.

Secret number 27

Inspired people know they can be a source of inspiration to themselves

There is nothing greater in life than inspiration. If you can inspire people you are really fulfilling life, and the fulfilling of life is our goal.
Rukmini Arundale

Exposing ourselves to the inspiration of others usually awakens our own senses of inspiration and what we need to learn is to listen to our own inner voice to see what we are inspired to next. We get marching orders from inspiration, a call to action ourselves, not only to be the audience to other people's dreams but also to live our own. That inner voice is always calling us forward; but we may deny that voice, try to bury it or rationalise it away. But it's our friend and is showing us our direction.

Too often, though, we become experts at talking ourselves out of most inspired ideas. A few years ago I was travelling into London by underground, reading a giveaway magazine aimed at helping women find new jobs on their way to work on a Monday morning. This brilliant idea suddenly hit me, 'They need a career coach to write a column for them and I am the person to do that!' I was so excited by the idea and then within seconds doubts crept in. *If they wanted a career columnist, they'd already have one, besides they probably haven't even heard of me and anyway I can write books but probably can't write columns, it's a whole different skill set and even if I could write one or two I'd probably run out of ideas and let them down...*

Within minutes I had dismissed that idea and felt uninspired again. But I had enough awareness to realise what I'd done and suddenly realised what was going on for me. I was very attached to the outcome of them saying 'Yes' and I was afraid of rejection so, rather than be rejected by the magazine, I rejected myself! I feel sure you know that process. I think one of the major things that stops us acting on our best ideas is *over-attachment to the outcome*. Unless we have a guarantee of the outcome we want, we won't act. But attachment saps our power, even debilitates us. We need to be willing to act on the inner voice even though we don't know what the outcome is likely to be. If I am really honest, while I wanted them to say yes, I was also afraid of them saying yes.

So here's the secret: We can become a source of inspiration to ourselves.

Then I got to thinking *how do I know whether they are interested or not? Let me find out.* So the next day I found the name of the editor, sent him a book and some material and then followed it up with a couple of telephone calls. As yet, I am not writing a column for them, although I now write columns for other magazines, so it obviously sowed a seed; but I just noticed how good I felt about myself for following through on my inspired idea with little attachment to the outcome. I had inspired myself by following through on what I knew I wanted to do but on which I was afraid to follow through. I took action in the face of my fears. How could you act in the face of your fear today?

Secret number 28

Inspired people know the power of passion

Passion is what we are most deeply curious about, most hungry for, will most hate to lose in life. It is the most desperate wish we need to yell down the well of our lives. It is whatever we pursue merely for it's own sake, what we study when there are no tests to take, what we create though no one may ever see it. It matters most whether we are doing it or not.
Gregg Levoy, author of *Callings*

I love the story of the perfumier Jo Malone. She was always passionate about smells and fragrances, describing her early childhood memories as snapshots in scents and smells rather than sights or sounds. She worked in a flower shop for a while, explaining 'I loved it, the smells as you cut the stems, that fresh green note. I learned the names of flowers, I would memorise them. I could name every lily, it was magical.' Jo's mother gave facial treatments in London to the rich and famous and made her own creams and, as time went by, Jo got more involved. When she began taking over after her mother became ill, Jo developed more of her own fragrances and attracted an international celebrity client list. But the clients wanted the fragrances too, separately from the facial treatment, so she started making them at night in her flat.

After 10 years of being in business and battling breast cancer, Jo's business is a multi-million pound success. She says, 'Starting my business was a journey of passion and love. It wasn't about playing it safe; there were failures along with success. My aim was for the brand to become the best, something I strive to maintain. Looking back, I've travelled the rough path of an entrepreneur but I have absolutely no regrets.' It was her own passion for what she loved that created a new audience. Until she innovated, people didn't know they wanted these fragrances. Julia Cameron, author of *The Artist's Way*, explains, 'Since each of us is one-of-a-kind, the market, for all its supposed predictability, is actually vulnerable to falling in love with any of us at any time.' And that is precisely what happened for Jo Malone; the world fell in love with her fragrances. When we are truly inspired we discover that our passion attracts and astonishes people.

So here's the secret: Inspired people know that we are rewarded in proportion to the passion we have for what we do.

Section five:
Reinforcing inspiration

We can learn to transform inspiration from a single event to a regular habit. We need to reinforce it again and again.

Secret number 29

Inspiration needs reinforcement

As a single footstep will not make a path on the earth, so a single thought will not make a pathway in the mind. To make a deep physical path, we walk again and again. To make a deep mental path, we must think over and over the kind of thoughts we wish to dominate our lives.
Henry David Thoreau

Can you relate to this experience? Have you ever got really inspired, felt truly clear and powerful but then gradually lost that connection and sunk down again? I think it's familiar for many of us. I know many people who have had peak experiences and become inspired to change their world but never quite got around to it. I was one of them. We become alight but then the fire goes out. How do we keep the fire alight? How do we make inspiration stick?

It's vital that we understand the difference between inspiration and motivation. We don't have to make ourselves inspired, it's naturally there; it's the divine fire within us and, like any fire, as we feed, protect and nourish it, it will keep burning. Inspiration then naturally draws us forward in our lives. Motivation is often more something that we try to impose on ourselves, it's more a force of *should* or *ought* or *must* or out of the fear of the consequences of not doing something. When that is our greatest motivation, it's likely to run out regularly because it's unsustainable. Only inspiration is sustainable. The goal is to motivate ourselves through inspiration rather than forcing ourselves or imposing on ourselves. It's easy for uninspired people go on a workshop or read a book and then believe, '*It didn't work.*'

Living an inspired life is a lot like learning a new language; we don't take a holiday or pick up a book of grammar and then expect to become fluent in Greek. It's a gradual process, learning some fundamentals to build on before we go on to the more advanced stuff. Same with inspiration but even more involved as inspiration is also a process which involves both learning and unlearning. To a great extent, getting new ideas is not the problem for many of us; the biggest problem is clearing our mind of the old ideas, beliefs and attitudes that hold us back.

So we need to reinforce inspiration and positivity daily. I heard it said that *I'll remember that* is the devil's whisper. We will forget important and crucial insights, so we need to remind ourselves. Remember, inspiration is not vaccination; we need it regularly. Most of us have had a lifetime of negative conditioning—an evening talk, a weekend seminar or one great book can inspire us but it is not going to undo the years of negativity that we have accumulated all in one go. That is the daily work of gradual personal transformation; it is the process of growing ourselves or, more precisely, revealing the true nature that already exists in embryo within us. We each become a different person as we follow our inspiration; we grow in consciousness, get lifted beyond the limiting sense of ourselves with which we grew up and discover ourselves to be greater persons by far than we ever dreamed ourselves to be. But inspiration is like a muscle, it needs to be built gradually, as one trip to the gym won't do it.

So here's the secret: We need to get inspired over and over again; it needs to become a habit, not an event.

Secret number 30

Inspired people know the difference between talking and being

We don't get wet thinking about water.
Alan Watts, spiritual teacher

I was just finishing a ten-day trip working in the South of Africa. I had started in Johannesburg, then gone to Maputo in Mozambique and was finally leading an event in Gaborone, capital of Botswana. Although I was tired from a hectic schedule, I felt a deeper disquiet within me but I wasn't sure what was going on. There I was doing the things I loved, teaching about inspiration and creativity, living my purpose. What was wrong? I emailed Barbara from the conference centre in Gaborone and explained rather sheepishly, 'I am a bit embarrassed to say this but I am feeling a little fed up with talking about inspiration and creativity. How can I be bored with inspiration?' The next day I got a response from her that made me understand what was going on. She responded, 'Yes, talking about inspiration and creativity is not the same as being inspired and creative.'

It was so obvious but it hadn't dawned on me. Talking about what I love and doing and being what I loved were different. I love talking and presenting but not all the time. I also need to balance that with quiet times, renewal times and alone times where I simply write and be creative. Whilst I understood the insight, I still felt uncomfortable. It wasn't until the following week when I was settled back in London and I had the time to sit down and do some inner listening, that I discovered my next assignment—this book! Ideas were bubbling up in my consciousness and, as I started to write, I felt something happening within me. I have never injected drugs but I imagined that I was experiencing what it must be like. As I started to write, as I was *being* creative, I felt different, an alchemy happened, like spiritual blood started coursing through my veins. I began to feel my spirits lifting and felt like I was becoming connected to myself again. It was mysterious but palpable; I began to feel at peace with myself and the discomfort began to evaporate.

I believe that inspiration has a physical effect; it renews our physiology. Inspiration becomes biology, as much unhappiness becomes biology. You've probably heard lots of stories about people who develop a life-threatening illness and are given six months to live. They throw in their jobs and begin to pursue their dreams and do what inspires them but what they've resisted doing. So they start painting, create the animal sanctuary, join the choir. But then a strange thing happens. Their illness goes into remission, they forget to die. As Stephen Pressfield ponders in *The War of Art,* 'Could it be that our unlived lives turn against us?' and maybe when we give it expression, it becomes our ally again?

So here's the secret: Inspired people don't just talk about dreams, inspiration and creativity, they give them expression, they *are* them, at least somewhere in their lives.

Secret number 31

Inspired people regularly put themselves in the presence of inspiration

Almost the whole world is asleep. Everybody you know, everyone you see, everyone you talk to. Only a few people are awake and they live in constant total amazement.
From the movie *Joe Versus the Volcano*

I believe in energy fields; I think everything vibrates at a particular frequency. Everything, especially people, has a presence and a radiance. I think something mysterious and yet tangible happens when we put ourselves in the presence of inspirational energy—it rubs off on us. When I went to hear Phillip Pullman speak, (Mentioned in *Secret Number 5*), I knew at the end of the 45-minute programme that I had been in the presence of a master of his craft. It wasn't just what he said, it was *how he was*. I have no aspirations or desire to be a writer of children's fiction but, as I crossed the Thames over Hungerford Bridge on my way to catch my train home, I was amazed to have several ideas for my own writing and my own business. Simply being in his presence had activated something in me and made me resonate at a new frequency.

Inspiration is a frequency to which we can learn to stay tuned and we do that by putting ourselves in the physical presence of inspiration. We can do this by going to seminars, concerts, plays, readings, recitals and displays. If there wasn't something magical about live concerts, why would we go to them? We might as well stay at home and listen to the CDs. Why do hundreds of people go to plays or musicals when we can stay at home and watch them on DVD? We do get some of the magic through recordings but obviously it is because there is a magic about being physically present, being in that energy of the performer or speaker. I have seen Bruce Springsteen live several times and know that there is an energy about his live presence that no recording can convey.

So here's the secret: Get yourself in the physical presence of inspirational energy regularly.

When we are in the presence of inspiration, something in us becomes rewired, our inner circuitry is altered. Something is awakened in us. Sometimes I think we limit ourselves to think that we can only learn from and be inspired by people who are doing what we are doing. Inspired people know that they can even learn from and be inspired by people totally unrelated to their business or creative activity.

Secret number 32

Inspired people know it can take so little to be inspiring

We achieve the great task by a series of small acts.
Tao Te Ching, Chinese philosophy

Inspired people know that if they keep raising the bar and looking to create big gestures of inspiration, they can easily end up doing nothing. Inspiration is often in the little and spontaneous stuff that we have the courage to do every day. I heard about Johnny Barnes from a friend who had just returned from visiting her brother in Bermuda. Johnny rises early at 4:45 am each morning to greet thousands of motorists on their way to work at Trimingham Hill roundabout in Hamilton, Bermuda. Come rain or shine you'll always see him smiling and he has become known as the friendliest man in Bermuda, telling people every morning, 'Good morning!' 'I love you!' and 'God bless!' Some drivers stop to shake Barnes's hand. Some present him with flowers. Others simply return the smile and wave. In any case, Barnes knows that he has succeeded once again in spreading joy.

So here's the secret: Inspired people know how simple and easy inspiration can be.

It all started back in 1983. Barnes, then 60, lived in Paget and worked at the bus depot in Hamilton as a driver and repairman. On his way to work one morning he had what can only be described as an epiphany. He stopped at the roundabout and began calling out to passers-by. At first, people thought he was crazy. Then, as they continued to see him morning after morning, they began to appreciate his joy and perseverance. When he was still a bus driver, he could only manage an hour but, now he's retired, he can continue until 10am. Barnes now shows up at the roundabout each morning with a bagged breakfast, a portable radio and a knapsack full of postcards of himself that he sells to tourists for $1 each. Sometimes he joins hands with tourists to pray for their safe journeys. Most commuters say they enjoy seeing Barnes each day as he helps them to face another day of stress and hard work and he makes the morning traffic easier to bear. Many people actually go out of their way to work so they can see him!

A few years ago, the Spirit of Bermuda Trust raised funds and commissioned a local sculptor to create a bronze statue of this Bermuda icon. His portrait adorns Hamilton's Visitor Service Bureau and he's been honoured by Her Majesty Queen Elizabeth II. Let's never forget how simple it is to be inspiring, Johnny Barnes has become world famous for waving, smiling and for spreading joy!

Secret number 33

Look for inspiration in unexpected places

People are like stained glass windows: they sparkle and shine when the sun is out but when the darkness sets in their true beauty is revealed only if there is a light within.
Elizabeth Kubler-Ross, author and teacher

Inspired people know that inspiration is often found in places where we would least expect to find it. A couple of days after arriving in Johannesburg my colleague, Richard, explained to me that on Monday we were going to visit Sidwell Nxumalo, 'Sid,' a friend of his who lived in Soweto, and Richard said I'd find Sid inspiring. Now, my only images of Soweto were of violence, burnings and shootings, so I remained to be convinced but trusted Richard, as he'd been there before. Officially just over a million people live in Soweto but unofficial estimates put it at more like four million and growing daily. It's busy and crowded but better than I thought it would be, although I was still concerned for my own safety. As we approached Senokonyeana Street in Orlando West, Soweto, there was spirit—we passed the world's largest murals painted on the side of Orlando Power stations. But I heard the words I least wanted to hear from Richard's mouth which were; 'Nick, I think we're lost'. A quick call to Sid's mobile and we were on track again and, as we approached and entered the Ubuntu Kraal that Sid created, it was as if we had entered an oasis. Even in the darkest days of apartheid, Sid had wanted to create something beautiful for the community.

Sid explained to me, 'The word *ubuntu* is a Zulu word and translates roughly as *humanity towards others*. But it means much more than this. The spiritual foundation of African societies, *ubuntu* involves a belief in a universal bond of sharing that connects all of humanity, a unifying worldview best captured by the Zulu maxim *umuntu ngumuntu ngabantu*— "a person is a person through other persons".' I wondered if apartheid had been motivated by the very opposite, to dehumanise and disconnect.

Sid had managed to become the first black master builder in South Africa and, using his contacts and resources, managed to buy an ash dump from the government. Over a period of 20 years he had literally transformed this ash dump into the sanctuary in which I was now standing. It was a green, lush and beautiful oasis. There was a conference centre, community centre, a place for weddings, a swimming pool, kitchens, beautiful flowers, birds. I was astonished. He loved his community so much he wanted to create something beautiful for it. I then discovered that Sid has helped dozens of other people in Soweto start their own small businesses. Later, as he drove us around it became obvious that he was a known and loved leader of his community but had chosen not to go into politics as he believed he could achieve more without those encumbrences. He showed us the only street in the world where two Nobel peace prize winners had lived—Desmond Tutu and Nelson Mandela—and drove us past their houses.

We drove back to the centre and thanked Sid for his time and care and, as we all hugged each other, another thought struck me. Richard had been in the army, so during apartheid Richard was responsible for implementing it. Fifteen years ago these two men in front of me hugging each other as brothers were enemies across a divide of colour; today they were friends in building a new country together. I was touched, moved and inspired, in Soweto! I learned that over 20% of the people that visit South Africa now visit Soweto, around 250,000 people a year, and it sets trends in politics, fashion, music, dance and language.

So here's the secret: Inspired people know that when they have the eyes to see it, they can find inspiration anywhere.

Secret number 34

Inspired people border on the obsessive

Don't fight forces, use them.
R. Buckminster Fuller, scientist and innovator

The ego is very prone to addictions and these addictions are often destructive of our lives; but they needn't be. I remember listening to the spiritual teacher Deepak Chopra talk once and he said, 'I have an addictive personality, so I may as well be doing something useful with it, like teaching, writing and helping people.' I felt very affirmed by his piece of self-disclosure. I had often been almost embarrassed and ashamed of my need to read spiritual and personal development books, listen to audios and be around positive people. I wondered what was wrong with me. Addictions are things we need and are dependent upon and we often dislike being dependent on anything. But the more I have got to know creative and inspired people, I recognise that they have a passion that almost borders on the obsessive for things that uplift them. They simply can't get enough of them. They are dependent on inspiration to lift them up.

So here's the secret: Put our addictive tendencies towards a positive goal—keeping our souls aloft.

Inspired people get to recognise this as a healthier need rather than a problem. We somehow take it as normal that we listen to negativity and bad news through the media every day but there is something wrong with us or we are slightly suspect because we have a need to keep our souls aloft! How strangely we have created this world! If we need to obsess about something, let it be about inspiration. To transform our consciousness, we need lots of good input. We've had ideas of lack and scarcity programmed into us for most of the day for most of our lives, so that takes a lot of undoing. If we aren't using our minds consciously, someone else will be trying to influence our thinking and attitudes.

The most important part of us is the mind, which is not the same as the brain. When one cares for one's mind, makes friends with it, always feeds it healthy food, engages it in positive activity, exercises it with knowledge and wisdom, one is rewarded. Like a garden returns fragrance and beauty according to the care invested, so the mind will repay us with thoughts, ideas and visions of great beauty when tended and invested with care. Where the mind goes, we go. What one's mind creates becomes one's destiny.

Secret number 35

Inspired people have heroes and heroines

The purpose of heroes and heroines is to remind us of all that can be achieved with inspiration, determination and passion
Anon

One of the phenomena I have noticed in my coaching practice is that when I suggest people spend more time around and in the presence of creative, inspired, purposeful and successful people, most people give me a strange look and tell me, 'I don't know any.' Neither did I, until I got involved with Alternatives. I got to think about how my life was positively influenced by having heroes and heroines, not only by getting to meet some of them but also seeking out and learning from people who represented and lived what was possible rather than arguing for their own limitations.

When we have the desire to look and have the eyes to see them, we will discover we live in a world where there are thousands of positive role models, living and historical. We can read about them, listen to them, meet some of them, study some and see the trail they have left so that we can be wiser for their experience. Role models show us what is possible for us; we learn what challenges they encountered and shaped their characters. We can learn from the wisdom that they have developed through their life experience and use it to avoid mistakes of our own.

So here's the secret: Become a detective. Discover and collect stories of your heroines and heroes. Here's the trick—use their lives to ennoble your own and recognise your own greatness, not to make yourself feel small.

We also need to expand the areas in which we have inspirational role models. Here are just a few ideas to look out for inspiring role models: spirituality, personal development, charitable work, entrepreneurialism/commerce, service to the community, courage and heroism, government, sporting achievement, creativity, film making, writing/literature, the media. Sometimes we have lots of heroes in some areas and very few in another, so we need to go and trawl for inspiration in specific areas.

Inspired people don't try to copy their heroes and heroines but learn from them. Successful people will offer to sell you the *secrets* that have made them successful but these programmes can't always deliver on the promises because the implicit message is 'Do what I've done and you will get the results that I've gotten.' That's an action-based, formulaic model. It completely leaves out the factors of individual inspiration, experience and desire. Inspired people don't *bolt on,* they take the experience of others and use it creatively in their own lives, in their own way, making it uniquely theirs.

Secret number 36

Inspired people learn to celebrate success

Bless the good that befalls others. No one else's good can take away from yours; the success of another is your own. The more you rejoice in the happiness of others, the more you rejoice in your own.
Alan Cohen, spiritual teacher

I am a great fan of *Cirque du Soleil*, the Canadian Circus troupe, and recently I went to see them at the Royal Albert Hall in London. Helen and I were there for their second night and, as we waited in our seats for the show to start, I found a review of the first night in the London *Evening Standard*. Whilst the reviewer praised the talent of the individual performers, I was saddened to read in the second paragraph, 'There is something soulless about the fact that they are now so successful there are umpteen shows running from Las Vegas to Manchester.' Read that statement again. What message is he giving? Success equals soulless. I have seen *Cirque* in London and Las Vegas and they are so full of spirit, incredible human talent honed through years of apprenticeship and inspiring performances. That is why they are so successful! And yes, they are now a £500 million business employing 3,000 people with 11 different shows; five of those shows tour the world, four shows are permanent in Las Vegas and a fifth will be added in 2006.

The reviewer was voicing an opinion that is so prevalent around success—that only struggling artists have soul and virtue and that by definition, as soon as we become successful, we must lose our hearts, souls and inspiration. It also demonstrates another core belief that many of us have taken on board—that success is bad and somehow not to be celebrated. When people become successful we want to knock them, bring them down a peg or two. That highlights a big fear that creates resistance in our subconscious mind that shows up in our own lives—why would we want to become successful if we are going to get knocked down and criticised? So we often hold ourselves back from success.

So here's the secret: When we celebrate success and talent, our own and others, we'll have more of it. Success is created *through* heart and soul.

Inspired people let the success of others lift them up and show them what is possible. They know that success is an abundant resource and that the more each of us is successful, the more it inspires those around us. Life is like a big puzzle with a unique shape cut out for every living being. The wonder and the miracle comes as each of us finds our own true place; we form the pattern for each of us to find our own places. We serve each other most powerfully by finding our own places. What we see in others, we affirm in ourselves. When we see the beauty and talent in others, we will find it in ourselves. Rachel, one of my friends, went to see a *Cirque* show in London and described to me how she was standing on the balcony when she saw the high wire performer and tears started to stream down her face. She said, 'I felt an urge to do *my* soul's work; it was like coming home.' She is now a clown professionally.

Section six:
Growing into prosperity

Inspiration calls us to grow spiritually and, as we do grow spiritually, it wants us to upgrade our quality of life

Secret number 37

Inspiration wants us to prosper and our lives be upgraded

There is a natural law of abundance which pervades the entire universe but it will not flow through a doorway of belief in lack and limitation.
Paul Zaiter

Many of us have grown up with one of two beliefs: either we have to sell our souls to make money and live in this world or we can follow our heart, be inspired and creative but the price we'll have to pay is being poor. Very few of us were bought up believing the truth, the third way—that when we are inspired and creative, we can prosper too; indeed, we are called spiritually to prosper. Our spirits want us to lift ourselves up so that we can prosper but our conditioning acts as ballast, weighing us down, keeping us afraid and worrying about survival rather than flourishing. Inspiration wants to upgrade our lives so that we can prosper on all levels: emotionally, spiritually, creatively, financially and materially.

So here's the secret: Inspiration calls us to be more and have more.

Remember, inspiration wants us to raise our sights, not lower them; it wants us to have better lives in all areas. It's not an overnight process but a dozen daily choices to make our lives more beautiful, uplift our minds and lift our energy higher; and there are a thousand ways we can do that as we align with the spirit within us. We must have the consciousness for that which we desire. Without the consciousness, it cannot come to us. With the consciousness, it must come. It's about changing our minds and then changing our lives. I think it safe to assume that the Muse is a being of beauty and high energy, so the higher we raise our energy, and have our lives reflect that energy, the more welcome the Muse will feel and the more inclined to visit. So how do we put the welcome mat out for the Muse?

It's a case of inner and outer reflecting each other. Our thoughts can be on Heaven but, if our home or office is a mess, there is chaos and disorder and the Muse will not be amused. She doesn't want to soil her dress. Have fresh flowers, beautiful quotations, objects of inspiration, incense and candles, create order, fix things that are broken, get yourself all you need to function so that your energy can go into creation, not frustration. I bought myself a huge new desk a year ago, the most beautiful I ever had since I became self-employed. As I unwrapped and assembled it, the thought came to me, *Big desk, big ideas.* I feel so much better when I sit down to work and create now. The Muse cares about beauty and is attracted by it.

Secret number 38

Inspired people know that their lives become a campus

We should, and can, produce riches in our own consciousness at the same time we are producing riches in the world. The more we do outwardly with our talent and power, the more we will grow inwardly in talent and power.
Edmond Bordeaux Szekely

Until we get inspired and start acting, we have no idea what we are capable of; but we don't discover what we are capable of until we start creating our dreams. Inspired people regularly do things that are new to them and they continually pioneer in their own lives, moving into new territory. Some of our talents are only liberated through inspiration and some great purpose. Uninspired people worry a lot about how things are going to work out, how success will be guaranteed. We want to have learned everything in advance and have our journeys be about applying what we already know. Inspired people care about that, too, but they also know that they learn the *how* as they go. We don't know everything before we start and we don't need to, we just need to know enough to take the first steps. The beautiful quote by Patanjali at the beginning of this book reminds us, 'When you are inspired by some great purpose, some extraordinary project, all your thoughts break your bonds: your mind transcends limitations, your consciousness expands in every direction and you find yourself in a new, great and wonderful world.' Patanjali is telling us that as we follow our inspiration, we learn and are shown *how to* as we go. Answers are revealed, discoveries made and skills learned *as we travel on our journey.* We build up the confidence as we realise that ignorance needn't be a hindrance when we are willing learners. We discover we know more than we thought we did.

Patanjali then goes on to teach us that, as we follow our inspiration 'Dormant forces, faculties and talents become alive and you discover yourself to be a greater person by far than you ever dreamed yourself to be.' As we follow through our ideas, often in the face of our fears, new gifts and talents arise within us. We learn how to do things as we start doing them. When we are inspired we do still learn a lot but this tends to be less by formal learning and more through countless *aha* moments, through revelation, insights, through reading about and studying other inspired people, through our own experiences and the successes and failures of peers and role models. Our lives become our campuses and our classrooms, living, learning journeys, unfolding and evolving daily.

So here's the secret: Inspired people are not intimidated by not knowing *how to*. They know they will have insights, learn and grow as they need to as they follow their inspiration.

Inspired people usually become very skilful at what they do; often not through a PhD or MBA but through life experience and by being apprenticed to their own *inner teacher*. In fact *A Course in Miracles* asks, 'Would you be willing to give up being your own teacher?' Encoded within inspiration is a spiritual teacher, an individual curriculum designed for us and our own growth, returning us to love and releasing us from fear. We can learn to become good students.

Secret number 39

Inspired people question their sources of advice

When embarking upon a journey, do not consult someone who has never left home.
Jalaludin Rumi, mystic poet

Our dreams are fragile and precious and often have trouble surviving the severe scrutiny of others. Too often we share an inspired idea with someone who is very happy to give us a number of problems with our idea and tell us why they are sure it won't work. Often this feedback crushes us and squashes our dream, especially when the source of advice is someone who we respect and care about.

To maintain our inspiration, we need to develop a very clear discernment. I recommend a mantra that you should drill into your consciousness and pull out frequently whenever offered advice—*consider the source*. Living an inspired life, we are going to find ourselves offered endless advice and unlimited opinions. The questions we should always ask are *Is this person living their own dreams? Do they have positive experience to base this on? Should I really be listening to them?* I never cease to be amazed at how many people listen to the advice and opinions of people who have no relevant experience and are often disgruntled Dreambuilders themselves.

So here's the secret: Inspired people always consider the source of advice when evaluating it.

Too often we give our power away to other people, trusting them more than ourselves. To stay inspired we need to build powerful mental filters—to let in good, life-affirming advice and experience and to keep out erroneous advice and opinion that is spirit-squashing—and to discern the difference between the two.

Secret number 40

Inspired people also learn *how to* when necessary

In a world that is constantly changing, there is no one subject or set of subjects that will serve you for the foreseeable future, let alone for the rest of your life. The most important skill is to acquire now is learning how to learn.
John Naisbit, author of *Megatrends*

When we are inspired, we want to become really good at what we do which leads us to want to develop our skills and become masterful. To do that we will need to learn skills and develop our *know how* but we'll be motivated differently from the way in which we would be if we *had* to learn. I once heard Anita Roddick, *Body Shop* founder, explain that at one time in her business she would never take on an MBA student for her business. She loved to recruit for passion and then train for skills but she couldn't train for passion and motivation.

The combination of inspiration and skills makes us extremely potent. If we don't have skills, we could become an inspired fool! So, just as inspired people know from whom *not* to accept advice, they also seek out masters of their craft from whom they *can* learn a lot, to whom they really *should* listen.

We also learn what we do need to know and we *don't* need to know. I remember many years ago learning how to fill in my VAT tax returns every quarter, even though my heart sank at the prospect of doing it. Then one day I asked my accountant if she had a book-keeper who could do my VAT return for me. I discovered that for £50 a quarter, I could be free of that that task! Just because we may work for ourselves doesn't mean that we need to do it all ourselves. As inspired people our jobs are to keep our energy high and to let other people, who love doing them, carry out your energy-draining tasks.

So here's the secret: Inspired people learn what they need to know and what they don't need to be good at.

Secret number 41

Inspired people know there is wisdom in failure

We are not taught how to fail and how to lose with dignity and awareness. Our so-called and imagined failures become the doorway to profound success in our lives—success that is not measured by commonplace standards but by the currency of depth of being, compassion and wisdom. In fact, failure and loss have the possibility to be among humanity's greatest tools for a process of radical internal transformation that is deeply satisfying as well as enduring.
Mariana Caplan, author of *The Way of Failure—Winning Through Losing*

Most people live their lives in fear of rejection and failure. Inspired people don't like fear, rejection or defeat, either but they develop the wisdom to know that the only way to avoid them are to say nothing, do nothing and risk nothing—and that is an unappealing option. Inspired people know that failure is not a reason to stop, it's not our undertaker and indeed can be a spectacular teacher. It can hurt badly, it can be humiliating but it gets our attention; it makes us think, feel, focus, question and ask for help.

We have to sit back and look hard at failure, learn from our mistakes, understand and transform them into wisdom. Inspired people know that with wisdom, failure is not a block to success but can be a doorway to success. What we are judging as failure may be as simple as lack of patience for something that isn't happening as fast as our expectations. Defeat can serve as well as victory to open our souls and let our glory out. In Silicon Valley, California, I read that more and more failure is not regarded as a black dot but a badge of achievement, showing that you were in the game, being innovative, daring, taking the knocks, engaging with life, taking risks and not sitting on the sidelines wondering.

So here's the secret: Even seeming failures are friends and teachers in disguise.

We live in society that worships success and shuns failure but failure is merely the shadow side of success; they are two sides of the same thing. Both are valuable and both are full of gifts. Inspired people learn to get beyond shame and denial around failure, to let it open them up to greater true humility and let it teach them. When we are honest with ourselves, we recognise that we have failed often and in many domains of life—both in concrete and subtle ways. There is also tremendous power in meeting head-on what we fear and have avoided; it no longer has as much power over us, we become liberated from it. When we integrate the power of what we've feared, its power is available *to* us.

Secret number 42

Inspired people understand the spiritual basis of prosperity

Perfectly wonderful people seem quite confused about whether prosperity should be considered a spiritual blessing. How relieved they are when shown that it definitely is! You need not be poor. It is a sin. Poverty is a form of hell caused by man's blindness to God's unlimited good for him. You should be prosperous, well supplied and have an abundance of good because it is your divine heritage. Besides, you can't be much good to yourself or to anyone else unless you are prosperous.
Catherine Ponder, author of *Prosperity Secrets of the Ages*

Inspired people understand that the belief that we should be poor and virtuous is a misunderstanding, an erroneous but widely-held belief that stops so many people succeeding with their own talents and creativity. Inspiration leads us to become more spiritual and being spiritual means being prosperous, including money and material things. There is nothing holy about not being able to pay our bills and worrying all the time. Poverty often takes people away from their spirituality rather than leading them towards it, to cheat, lie or steal, causing them and others suffering. Just as we once thought the earth was flat but now laugh at that belief, in the future we will laugh at the belief that it was thought be unspiritual to prosper. We will all come to believe that the universe is fundamentally abundant and that the only shortages are created in our own minds which can be hosts for either prosperity or poverty.

Inspired people know that it is spiritual and holy to seek prosperity. A desire to be more prosperous is a divine desire, our creator tapping at our consciousness inviting us to upgrade our lives and the lives of all the people around us. We don't do this by self sacrifice, however; we do it through raising our own consciousness and then we can help the people around us. But it starts with us. To have more and share more, we must receive more; and to receive more, we need to become more. We must discover more of the spiritual self that we already are, and the innate gifts, talents and spirit within us.

Inspired people know that our creator's ability to help us prosper goes beyond market fluctuations, politics, lay-offs and shortages. There are no shortages in God's world. When we open ourselves to receive and give from the highest place within us, God transcends all Earthly laws for us to prosper.

So here's the secret: Inspired people are excited to prosper and demonstrate the ability we all have to flourish.

Secret number 43

Inspired people risk their significance

I choose to risk my significance.
To live so that that which comes to me as seed
Goes to the next as blossom
And that which comes to me as blossom
Goes on as fruit.
Dawna Markova

One of the great forms of resistance so many of us experience is that we battle against our own feeling of insignificance. We ask ourselves *Who am I to ... write a book; give advice; teach people; make a difference; confront a situation; express my feelings?* We may have grown up not feeling affirmed or being told we weren't that important or may have felt humiliated. This is one of the greatest blockers of creativity and talent. Inspired people are not immune to this and, in fact, probably experience it even more when they commit to move forward with their ideas.

When we don't believe in our significance, either we just don't bother to pursue our dreams or we try to overcompensate to prove that we are important when we don't really believe it. When we begin to know our own significance, our unconditional value, we move beyond competition. We don't have to become more important than anyone else, others aren't threats to us, because we are rooted in knowing our own value.

So here's the secret: Inspired people are willing to risk their own significance.

Significance is not something that we can demand from the world but must find within ourselves. It was given to us by our Creator with our creation but we have forgotten. Our significance can be reinforced by feedback from others, for our achievements. The ultimate significance is simply being at peace with our selves and that who we are is significant. We have been bought into existence for a purpose by a living creator and we are loved unconditionally. We are not spare parts but an essential and necessary part of creation. *A Course in Miracles* tells us unequivocally, 'God Himself is incomplete without you. Without your joy, His joy is incomplete.' As Mother Teresa said, 'Everyone I see and serve is simply Christ in disguise.' We *are* that important to God and to Life.

Secret number 44

Inspired people invest in their own growth and learning

I've learned that following what you love magnifies your talent. You just have to have the faith to invest in it.
Leslie Rector

Inspired people fully understand the difference between cost and investment and choose to invest in themselves on an ongoing basis. They know that in the most positive way, they are always a work in progress, constantly growing and becoming. It's been calculated that most people spend vastly more on what they put *on* their heads through personal grooming than they ever spend on what they put *in* their heads through personal development and continued adult learning.

Be honest; do you consider yourself a good investment? If someone were to offer to invest money in you, would you be excited about the opportunity or anxious that you could fail them? There was recently a TV series on BBC2 in the UK called *Dragons Den* in which budding entrepreneurs had to pitch their business ideas to successful entrepreneurs (the 'Dragons') and ask them to invest their money in the new idea. In one show with 10 presentations, only one person got investment. Why? Either because they hadn't thought their idea through or they arrogantly demanded that other people invested in them when they wouldn't invest in themselves.

So here's the secret: Inspired people know they are worth investing in and they invest in themselves regularly before they expect others to.

Inspired people also know that they can build up confidence and self-belief *by* investing in themselves. Inspired people also have a fabulous level of discernment between when they are going on another course because they are afraid to take the next step with what they already know and when they are genuinely increasingly their knowledge and skills. They recognise that being a perpetual student, without also being a teacher, can be a fabulous form of resistance. The goal is to go as far as you can with what you already know *and* be regularly learning and developing.

Secret number 45

Inspired people embrace their own gifts

Your giftedness blesses the world, for the more you receive, the more you give. It is your joy to share your giftedness because it is a way of joining with others and creating a better world for everyone you come into contact with.
Dr. Chuck Spezzano

Quite simply, inspired people know that their gifts are one of the major ways to express their divinity on earth. A gift is different from a skill; a skill is something learned from the outside while a gift is remembered. Our gifts are innate, they are on the inside. We can also enhance our gifts by developing our skills. Inspired people know that gifts are what we naturally gravitate towards and spend time doing and being. It's what we do when no-one is watching or evaluating us.

We know the job is to discover what is already within us. The meaning of Life is to find our gifts, the purpose of Life is to share them freely. Conversely, when we have gifts and don't practise or share them, we diminish our own divine natures. If we truly exalted in our personal gifts, we could also celebrate the gifts of other people and the diversity of talents that God has given all of us. When we choose to honour our gifts, we participate in the recreation of this world. As we contribute our specific gifts and talents to the whole, so is each piece of the jigsaw puzzle of life put together forming the perfect picture.

So here's the secret: Inspiration awakens our gifts and talents, the things that flow easily from us.

Our uniqueness is our gift to the world. No two people have the same qualities, vision and experience and our life's work emerges from our own melting pot. We often miss our gifts because they are so natural and easy for us, they flow from us and who we are, so we don't consider that they can really be of value.

Section seven:
Inspiration and the higher realms

Just as resistance tries to squash our inspiration, there are higher levels of consciousness—Angels and Muses—cheering us on and actively supporting us.

Secret number 46

Inspired people understand the spirituality of their dreams

One dream reveals another, inspires another, prepares for another, unites with another and is shared with another to reveal this idea of God. This idea of God was established well before our first breath. We had nothing to do with its inception. It must be made manifest here on earth.
Helen Gordon, author of *All You Need Is Within You*

One of the greatest gifts of inspiration is that it points us to our dream; what most inspires us will be part of our creator's dream for us. Our inspired ideas and dreams are precious, often more precious than we realise, because they are divinely inspired, God-given. Each of us has a dream within our very soul that came with our creation, a dream we promised to fulfil in our lives; this dream is what will truly fulfil us and is often what we resist most. Our dream is partly about creating something but, as much as anything else, it is about becoming who we were born to be. Miracles happen when we give more energy to our dreams than our fears.

Our dream is our soul's urging to express itself which is also our divinity wanting to be expressed through us. Our dreams are not selfish, they are for our joy but, as we live from the most inspired place within us, our activities will inspire many who, in some way, have the opportunity to witness the joy of our lives and our work. Our inspired dreams can be a revelation to others, perhaps even revealing to them their own dreams, just as the inspiration of others will have been a revelation to us.

So here's the secret: Our truest dreams are divinely inspired and divinely supported.

Too often we try to control our dreams, not exposing them for fear of ridicule; but by ourselves we will not fulfil our dreams. Out of ego power we will most likely fail. It's a wonderful thought that our dreams are something impossible *until* we discover our greatest spiritual powers. Our dreams call us to partner with the divine within us, to partner with friends, family, loved ones, colleagues, customers and suppliers. We are all on the same team, whether we know it or not.

Secret number 47

Inspired people discover and serve their territory

In reality, we are servants of the Mystery. We were put here on earth to act as agents of the Infinite, to bring into existence that which is not yet, but which will be, through us.
Steven Pressfield, author of *The War of Art*

My friend Wendy was a little low and depressed and my partner Helen invited her to come share the market stall where she sold her jewellery and knitwear one Sunday. Within minutes of Wendy's arrival she had helped several stallholders set themselves up more beautifully, given a couple of psychic readings for people and was chatting away. From being unhappy, she had put herself in service; now she was happy and making money!

When we act divinely, our territory is revealed to us, we are shown how we can be in service to Life. Our territory is the place where we feel most in our element, where the soul feels at home. We nourish our territory and we are nourished by it. Territory is less about place and more about consciousness. Our territory is often born out of things with which we have struggled ourselves, been around on our own transformational journey and then returned to again with a gift for ourselves and our community. As we learn more, become creative and share our creativity, people will resonate with that and be drawn to us. As we share our gifts, our territory—our tribe—is drawn to us and we are attracted to it. There is a mutual seeking going on. We serve them and in doing so we are replenished. The more we replenish, the more we have share, so the journey becomes perpetually enriching. We learn to drill deeper into our understanding of ourselves and others.

So here's the secret: Inspired people know they serve Heaven, they are doing the Big Work, they serve Love.

My territory is work—bringing inspiration, creativity and meaning into it; after his own mental health challenges, my friend Rick's territory is helping people whose lives are a mess and feel like giving up; out of that he helps them create success; Mary runs a bed and breakfast in Glastonbury and her territory is connecting people to the sacredness of the landscape; my friend Ben's territory was helping teenagers create healthy relationships; for others it might be parenting, working with the homeless or children. That's our calling, to serve and be served by our territory. If we are religious, we'd call this our ministry.

We misunderstand service when we think it needs to be sad or soulless. It's about helping tsunami victims that have lost everything and we also serve Heaven by spreading joy. Patch Adams, the clown, doctor and social activist says, 'The unencumbered life of service is worth paying to do.'

Secret number 48

Inspired people are willing to be seen and known

One of the reasons I became successful was because I was willing to give up being anonymous.
Sophia Loren, actress

At one of our *Publish Your Book* seminars, one of the delegates said to us, 'I have got a great idea for a book but I am not going to write it because it would be so successful that I would become public and lose all my privacy.' I was a bit shocked. How did she know? Her concern may or may not have been a reality but to me it demonstrated a fear that many of us have—we are unwilling to be seen and known.

Inspired people often become willing to overcome their resistance to being known and seen. Many of us have mixed associations with having a lot of attention. We associate attention with disapproval, attack or jealousy. Part of us craves it and enjoys it and other parts of us may prefer to be less visible or even invisible and, of course, we can be both at different times. I know I got messages when I was young about 'Don't show off!' so both enjoyed and had uncomfortable feelings about too much attention. I remember hearing Richard Olivier speak once at Alternatives and, being a son of Laurence Olivier, the world's greatest actor, he knew a lot about fame and attention. Richard said, 'You can use fame to get your own needs met or you can use fame to bless people and help people.'

So here's the secret: Inspiration often invites us to be seen and known, so that we can make a positive impact.

Like everything, it's not so much the level of form that is important but the intention behind it. My belief is that each of us has gifts and talents that help and serve other people and it's our job to find lots of ways to share our gifts with other people, in ways that we'll enjoy and through which we'll prosper. If we have gifts that can help thousands but hide away, we rob ourselves and rob others. We may well have to learn about boundaries, how to say yes and how to say no with honesty and authority. We may also need to make peace with enjoying attention. It took me a while to acknowledge that sometimes I like being the centre of attention and to reach lots of people.

Secret number 49

Inspired people know they'll also have dark nights of the soul

There is a light that shines in each of us that does away with all darkness.
Jerry Jampolski and Diane Cirincione, authors and spiritual teachers

Inspired people know that sometimes the way to the mountaintop is through the valley. There are times when we are convinced that inspiration has run out, we'll never have a good day again and we've hit the wall, feeling there is no way forward. There are times when our inspiration leads us to a dark night of the soul, when old ways of doing and being no longer work and sometimes we are bought to our knees in pain and despair. Hope, purpose and meaning can run out. Painful as it is, it is also a renewal. Our personality thought it wanted a makeover but the Holy Spirit decided we needed new foundations, so it brings out the wrecking ball. We are taught to avoid pain, not to let it be our teacher. In the midst of the dark nights of the soul, the holy surgeon is cutting away the dead wood of the personality, letting it die so that a new part of our spirit can be reborn. In Buddhism, this is the path to freedom, dying while we are alive. We go through a transformation and rebirth.

In the Kabbalah, the Jewish mystic tradition, it teaches that sometimes we have to go down in order to gather the energy to leap up. This isn't spirit being cruel, it isn't a punishment but loving us in uncompromising ways. Spirit doesn't want to humour the ego, it wants to dissolve it, a layer at a time, so that the real Self is revealed. Spiritual teacher Ram Dass had a major stroke and nearly died and is still rehabilitating. He made a film about how blessed he was beginning to feel about the whole experience. He called the film *Fierce Grace*. Grace indeed can be fierce; we need to let go of that which is not love and, if we don't do it willingly, we may need to be dragged into it kicking and screaming. We may need to let go of broken dreams so we can have new life. New and greater life is always being offered to us. As the mystic poet Kabir says,

'What have I ever lost by dying?' The light is always present and pulling us forward, even when we can't see it or feel it.

So here's the secret: Inspired people are willing to encounter their own darkness and bring light to it.

Secret number 50

Inspired people know that ease *isn't* cheating but is natural

The Bible has taught us, metaphysics has taught us, myth has taught us, that if you get into the flow, if you do what you're supposed to do, you'll be rewarded with riches you've never imagined. And so what I have received is the natural order of things. You always, always, always reap what you sow.
Oprah Winfrey, Television show host

A coaching client came to me because she'd taken early retirement from a news-gathering agency in London to pursue some other interests, including something she had trained in called *Spontaneous Story Telling*. She was passionate about it but never brought her ideas for running workshops to fruition. I had a hunch that, given her Scottish protestant background, a dynamic was at work. I asked her, 'Do you take what you love and turn it into hard work?' She smiled a great expression of recognition and said, 'I hadn't thought of that but I guess I do. When I was growing up I was told that everything had to be hard work if it was to become successful.'

Do you remember at school being given your report and you got marks for effort and attainment? Attainment was what we achieved, effort was how hard we tried. So even if we didn't succeed, we could get lots of recognition for trying hard. Rarely do we get medals or certificates for ease and grace, only for struggle and sacrifice. For many of us this carries over to our adult lives where we seek recognition for how hard we tried, how much struggle we had, even if we didn't achieve anything. We may either take *trying hard but not succeeding* and turn it into an art form or we may make things more difficult for ourselves than necessary in order to justify and earn our success.

Inspired people know that success doesn't need to be earned, deserved or struggled for, it simply needs to be chosen, created and allowed for. The goal of being inspired is that life is supposed to flow more, to become easier and more natural. Through inspiration we can transform emotional drama into genuine excitement and the joy of growth. But often the old protestant work ethic is so strong in us that we automatically take what we love, what inspires us, and create struggle and difficulty with it. We are so habitually addicted to struggle that we don't realise there is an easier option and we may well even be suspicious of anything that is easy or feels too good, believing that it can't be useful or of any real value. The struggle and difficulty may even be a large part of our identity; we don't know who we'd be without struggle. We might lose the nobility of our suffering. One purpose of inspiration is to invite us to natural self-expression, being ourselves and authentic, not struggling to be anything other than who and what we are.

So here's the secret: Inspiration wants things to be easy for us, if we let it.

Like the Bible quote about the lilies of the field not needing to struggle, neither do we. We struggle when we go against our true natures and we experience ease when we act naturally, from the heart. We can learn to turn down that sneaking voice that says you are cheating because it's easy, you should be suffering more. Many people have grown up believing that struggle entitles them to something from people who are doing better than they are. 'I have struggled, so I want my reward, my entitlement' but it doesn't work like that. Life is not going to reward us for our struggling and suffering but open up to us as we relinquish struggle.

Secret number 51

Inspired people know that ideas are centres of consciousness

The same Source that gave you the idea will give you the means to see it through.
Alan Cohen, author and spiritual teacher

How does inspiration change the world and our lives? Through ideas. Mind is the origin of everything and our lives, health, relationships and prosperity are all the result of the ideas we let take root in our mind. We can have ideas of lack, fear and scarcity and ideas of abundance, prosperity and plenty. Our minds can be host to both; the job is to become aware of the thoughts we are cultivating, nurturing the ones we want more of and weeding out the ones we want to diminish.

You may have heard the story about Cindy Cashman. She had an idea for a book called, *What Men Know About Women* which would be a book with a cover and blank pages! Her women friends loved the idea and giggled with delight, so she decided to create it. So far she has sold over one million copies of the book! If a great idea of a book with no words can be such a great success, how many other brilliant ideas are waiting within our consciousness? The Infinite mind is, well, infinite; there are no limits. Ideas are always entering the collective consciousness from the Infinite mind to us as individuals through inspiration and, when other people like your idea, resonate with it, are inspired by it or entertained by it, the idea takes off.

So here's the secret: Inspired people cherish ideas and understand their power.

Inspired people know that any lack in our lives is as a result of either not having enough great ideas or not fully following-through on the great ideas we have had. It's ideas that people resonate with and buy from us that create the money for us to pay our bills. Too often people have great ideas but dismiss them, resist them, don't know *how to* follow through or are afraid to follow through.

I am always fascinated to see the impact of ideas and stories like Harry

Potter, Star Wars, Mickey Mouse or James Bond. These characters don't actually exist but they exist within most minds on the planet as if they are people or beings. Their impact on the collective consciousness has been enormous. But they are still simply ideas and ideas live in our minds and then become manifest in the world.

Secret number 52

Inspired people understand the true nature of prayer

Prayer is not the overcoming of God's reluctance, but the taking hold of God's willingness
Phillip Brooks

The popular view of prayer is that it is the way us *poor and miserable sinners* beg God to give us something we need and, if we've been good and kept to the rules, maybe we'll be given some goodness. This totally misunderstands prayer. Inspired people have a different understanding of the purpose of prayer. We understand our significance, we know we are loved and important and that the Creator has already given us everything we need for happiness and fulfilment; nothing has ever been withheld from us or ever will be. The purpose of prayer then is to lift *our* minds up to that place where we know and experience that.

Inspired people know that the real question that determines the quality of our lives is not *how much can we steal, beg for or manipulate from God?* but *How much will we let God give us?* The function of prayer is to lift our souls to a new level, one aligned with our wellbeing and the purpose of our souls, so that our lives become renewed. We might be looking for a miracle, and they may come along the way, but the goal is to step into a new outlook that will bring greater clarity and effectiveness to all that we do. We can say that our prayers are effective only when we come to know ourselves and God more intimately and live in a new energetic vibration. Prayer is about our developing that consciousness that will attract all good things naturally—seeking the Kingdom first so that all can be added.

So here's the secret: Inspired people know God withholds nothing from them.

Inspired people know that God is withholding nothing from us, only we can withhold it from ourselves. The purpose of prayer is to dissolves the blocks in our mind so that our good can naturally come to us. God wants us to open the door to prosperity in our minds so that it can flow into our lives, for the benefit of our selves and others.

Secret number 53

Inspired people cherish stillness

When we set aside time each day for deep communion with the infinite then, as surely as day follows night, the light of inspiration will illuminate our beings.
Rev. Dr. Michael Beckwith

One of the great enemies of inspiration is excess busyness. Inspired people are usually active and engaged in the world and they also know that the quality of their activity is wonderfully enhanced when that activity is punctuated with stillness and silence, with white space. Silence and stillness are the root of our union with the divine, with ourselves and with one another. Mother Teresa reminds us, 'In silence we are filled with the energy of God Himself which makes us do all things in joy. The more we receive in silent prayer, the more we can give in our active lives.' Stillness is not an opposite of activity but the twin soul of it. Inspired people find comfort and renewal in silence and are not afraid to look within themselves because they know they will find goodness within them. Silence is not *nothing* but the place of all possibility in potential, the source which will always spring up if we search there.

So here's the secret: Inspired people treasure stillness.

When we think that only activity is productive, we are anxious if we aren't busy. However, the more we cherish stillness, the more we find that as we slow down everything we were chasing starts to come to us. Stillness and immersing ourselves in silence recharges the spiritual batteries and, in doing so, makes us attractive, more of a magnet. When we want new ideas, new inspiration, they will often come when we clear a space in our hearts and minds and, as the poet David Whyte reminds us 'Silence is the only way we will come to something new.' The quieter we become, the more we can hear. We often need to stop trying so hard and let another power work within us. We can learn from music, where *rest* is a musical term for a pause between flurries of notes. Without that tiny pause, the torrent of notes can be overwhelming. Without a rest in our lives, the torrents of our lives can be the same. Easily said, and inspired people give silence a priority, even when they are busy. As the soil renews itself during the wintertime so, when the mind is allowed to be quiet, it renews itself.

Secret number 54

Inspired people dream bold rather than argue for their limitations

Do not limit life to your beliefs. Instead, expand your beliefs to embrace all that life has to offer.
Alan Cohen, spiritual teacher

I recently had the pleasure of meeting Steven Pressfield, a personal hero of mine. He is the author of *The War of Art* (which I have quoted here), one of the best books ever written on overcoming our resistance to creativity, as well as author of *The Legend of Bagger Vance* which Robert Redford made into a Hollywood film, *Gates of Fire*, and several other novels. He agreed for me to interview him for a new venture that Terry Malloy, a friend of mine, has produced called *Closer to the Dream*, a monthly DVD magazine full of inspiring ideas, stories and interviews. Terry had left his secure job in banking to follow his heart and create this project and was both excited and insecure, as this was only the second day of filming.

Steven was generous with his time, his Malibu home and his heart and, as we were packing up the cameras and sound gear after the interview, Steven was chatting to Terry about *Closer to the Dream*. Steven said, 'I really think you are on to something there with the monthly DVD idea. Dream big and bold with it and don't let anyone limit you. Whoever you might want to interview, you can get to them, you just have to figure out how; but dreaming without limits is the key.' Now I don't know about you but I wished I'd had someone like that around me when I was growing up! I had so many messages about *don't be silly*, *who do you think you are?* and *be realistic*. I grew up learning about limitation, not possibility. Too often we spend our time and energy arguing for why we *can't* do something, wanting to be right that our limits are real, not self-created concepts. Our egos thrive on wanting to be right and we can put tremendous energy into trying to prove that something is impossible rather than making it happen. This is just another form of resistance, our fears being so strong that we are afraid to move beyond them. Inspiration always wants us to raise our sights, not lower them.

I know that Steven was not just being nice but talking from personal experience. He knew, deep down, that he was a writer at heart but struggled for over ten years before he even got published, his resistance was so strong, and many more years before he was able to make a good living as a writer. He knows limitation and he knows success. He knows that the only true limits are within us and our thinking, not in the world, and that the imagination is one the greatest powers we have. Steven's words were so powerful and affirming for Terry at the beginning of his project and like smelling salts to his soul.

So here's the secret: Inspired people dream bold and attract champions for their dreams.

The future belongs to the inspired

There is nothing sadder or more wasteful than untapped human potential and unexpressed human gifts. One's nature is to keep learning, growing and unfolding into who one was born to be. We were born for greatness, not mediocrity.
Nick Williams

Work is as important as family and relationships, it completes the triangle of human expression. Our whole lives are influenced by our relationships to our work. It's hard to hate work while loving marriage and family. Hating anything is poisonous to everything. When our work contains joy, adventure and creativity, our whole lives are lifted. I am passionate about liberating human talent—my own and that of other people. It is what transforms the world; sharing our gifts with each other is what makes our lives meaningful.

'*The Work We Were Born To Do* is about discovering our own unique gifts and personal destinies which are unlocked only by inspiration, not money. Inspiration is the key that unlocks true nature.

'My own story, from boredom and feeling under-utilised in corporate life to international speaker and author, uniquely qualifies me to talk with authority and authenticity about how to transform our working lives. I hope my journey of triumph over fear, self-doubt and low self-confidence will inspire you to discover the spiritual greatness that exists within you.'

For 15 years Nick has been inspiring people at work, helping them to discover their life's work and transform limiting beliefs and self-sabotaging behaviour into business and personal success. He is a much sought-after international speaker and has created a global family of friends living *The Work They Were Born To Do.*

Personal coaching and mentoring

with Nick Williams

Nick has already coached hundreds of people across the planet to greater success, creativity and fulfilment by helping them to discover the work they were born for and, for many, start their own inspired businesses.

Nick has limited availability for one-to-one coaching by telephone, e-mail and face to face.

To find out more about Nick and his coaching see www.nick-williams.com or contact him at nick@heartatwork.net

The Future Belongs to the Inspired

Nick Williams corporate and conference speaking

Nick's messages resonate with the corporate world and he is in demand as a speaker and trainer around the world in commercial companies and the charity sector. He is regularly invited to the USA, South Africa, Botswana, Mozambique, Barbados, Dublin and France as well as cities around the UK.

He is passionate about helping organisations become more inspired places in which to work and be, to liberate the talents and gifts of people in the workplace and to have workplaces be places of success without sacrifice.

His client list includes household names like BBC, BT, IKEA, W. H. Smith, PricewaterhouseCoopers, Yo Sushi, Pret A Manger, The Health and Safety Executive, The University of Westminster and The Royal College of Nursing, as well as many local authorities and NHS trusts.

To find out how Nick could contribute to your conference or company, and to find a list of testimonials, call 07000 781922, see www.nick-williams.com, or e-mail him on nick@heartatwork.net.

Books from Nick Williams

Powerful Beyond Measure (*Thorsons*)
This book is about a different kind of power. Inside us is a stirring, a remembering of a different kind of power that doesn't involve loss or domination. We are remembering our spiritual power, the power of love. **£7.99**

The Work We Were Born To Do (*Thorsons*)
Do you want a job that's creative, exciting and rewarding? That allows you to be who you truly are? You need to discover the work you were born to do. **£12.99**

The 12 Principles of the Work We Were Born To Do (*Sogna Bella/Tethered Camel*)*
Leading work-expert Nick Williams has identified the twelve principles of the work we were born to do. He shows how we can activate these principles to amazing effect and utilise our inner power at whatever stage we have reached in our working lives. A 128-page synopsis of the principles of *The Work We Were Born to Do* with extra exercises. **£6.99**

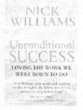

Unconditional Success (*Thorsons*)
For some people the very mention of the word 'success' brings to mind memories of challenges met and ambitions realised; for others, in contrast, this simple word can trigger feelings of inadequacy and failure, of much wasted energy and missed opportunities. **£7.99**

All these books are available from Heart at Work—just visit <u>www.nick-williams.com</u>

or send a cheque to Heart at Work, PO Box 2236, London W1A 5UA.